ALL-TIME AWESOME COLLECTION OF Good Clean Jokes FOR KIDS

Bob Phillips

HARVEST HOUSE PUBLISHERS
EUGENE, OREGON

Scripture quotations in this book are taken from the King James Version of the Bible.

Cover by Terry Dugan Design, Minneapolis, Minnesota

ALL-TIME AWESOME COLLECTION OF GOOD CLEAN JOKES FOR KIDS

Published by Harvest House Publishers
Eugene, Oregon 97402

Some material has been taken from Bob Phillips' books *Nutty Good Clean Jokes for Kids, More Awesome Good Clean Jokes for Kids, Ultimate Good Clean Jokes for Kids,* and *Crazy Good Clean Jokes for Kids!*

ISBN 13: 978-0-7369-1777-3
ISBN 10: 0-7369-1777-2
Product # 6917773

Printed in the United States of America

06 07 08 09 10 11 12 13 14 / BP-MS / 10 9 8 7 6 5 4 3 2 1

Contents

1

Nit: I hear that Margie and Harry had some hot words. Is it true?
Wit: Yes, she threw a bowl of alphabet soup at him.

Nit: What is easy to get into but hard to get out of?
Wit: I have no clue.
Nit: Trouble.

Nit: What is the difference between the world's heavyweight boxing champion and a man with a cold?
Wit: I don't know.
Nit: One knows his blows and the other blows his nose.

Nit: What does a real estate salesperson have to know?
Wit: Beats me.
Nit: Lots.

Nit: What shoemaker makes shoes without using any leather or rubber?
Wit: I can't guess.
Nit: A blacksmith—he makes horseshoes.

Nit: What kind of phone can make music?
Wit: I have no idea.
Nit: A saxophone.

Nit: What kind of beans do not grow in a garden?
Wit: You tell me.
Nit: Jelly beans.

Nit: What has a head, but can't think?
Wit: I give up.
Nit: A match.

Nit: What do giraffes have that no other animals have?
Wit: Who knows.
Nit: Little giraffes.

Nit: What kind of fish do you find in a bird cage?
Wit: You've got me.
Nit: A perch.

Nit: What color is a guitar?
Wit: My mind's a blank.
Nit: Plink!

Nit: Why did the little girl eat bullets?
Wit: That's a mystery.
Nit: Because she wanted to grow bangs.

Nit: What does the vegetable garden say when you tell it a joke?
Wit: I'm blank.
Nit: Hoe hoe hoe!

Nit: What would you call Batman and Robin if they were run over by a truck?
Wit: I don't have the foggiest.
Nit: Flatman and Ribbon.

Nit: What is worse than a giraffe with a sore throat?
Wit: It's unknown to me.
Nit: A centipede with blisters.

Nit: What letter is never found in the alphabet?
Wit: I'm in the dark.
Nit: The one you mail.

Nit: What letter is a vegetable?
Wit: Search me.
Nit: P.

Nit: What bird can lift the heaviest weight?
Wit: You've got me guessing.
Nit: A crane.

Nit: What has 18 legs and catches flies?
Wit: I pass.
Nit: A baseball team.

Nit: What country is useful at mealtime?
Wit: How should I know?
Nit: China.

Nit: What state serves as a source of metal?
Wit: I don't know.
Nit: Ore.

Nit: What letter is a part of the head?
Wit: I have no clue.
Nit: I.

Wit: Have you ever tried to tickle a mule?
Nit: No, why should I?
Wit: You'd get a big kick out of it.

Nit: The surgeon removed a healthy appendix with a blunt scalpel.
Wit: What a pointless operation!

Nit: What do you say to a tailor about his clothes?
Wit: I have no clue.
Nit: Suit yourself.

Nit: What do you say to a guy driving a car with no engine?
Wit: Beats me.
Nit: How's it going?

Nit: What did they do to the lady who stole some eye makeup?
Wit: I can't guess.
Nit: She got 50 lashes.

Nit: What's red and red and red all over?
Wit: I have no idea.
Nit: Measles with a sunburn.

Nit: Did you hear about the camper who swallowed the flashlight?
Wit: That's awful.
Nit: Yeah, he hiccuped with delight.

Nit: What did the wise old canary say to the parrot?
Wit: I give up.
Nit: Talk is cheep–cheep.

Nit: What do you call a bee that talks in very low tones?
Wit: You've got me.
Nit: A mumble-bee.

Nit: What do you get if you cross a porcupine with a peacock?
Wit: My mind is blank.
Nit: A sharp dresser.

Nit: What do you get when you cross a motorcycle with a joke book?
Wit: That's a mystery.
Nit: A yamahaha.

Nit: What do bank robbers like to eat with their soup?
Wit: I don't know.
Nit: Safe crackers.

Nit: What question do you always have to answer by saying yes?
Wit: I have no clue.
Nit: What does y-e-s spell?

Nit: Why do eggs go to the gym?
Wit: Beats me.
Nit: They like to eggsercise.

Nit: If you wanted to take a bath without water, what would you do?
Wit: I can't guess.
Nit: Sunbathe.

Nit: What happens to a person who lies down in front of a car?
Wit: I have no idea.
Nit: He gets tired.

Nit: What goes tick-tock woof?
Wit: I give up.
Nit: A watchdog.

Nit: What kinds of birds are kept in captivity more than any others?
Wit: Who knows?
Nit: Jailbirds.

Nit: What is both small and large at the same time?
Wit: You've got me.
Nit: A jumbo shrimp.

Nit: What kind of a bone should you not give to a dog?
Wit: My mind is blank.
Nit: A trombone.

Nit: What do you call a hot dog when it's in a bad mood?
Wit: That's a mystery.
Nit: A crankfurter.

Nit: What do they call the man who cuts the lion's hair?
Wit: I have no clue.
Nit: The mane man.

Nit: If you were invited out to dinner and found nothing on the table but a beet, what would you say?
Wit: I haven't the foggiest.
Nit: Well, that beet's all!

Nit: They were planning to add my brother's head to Mount Rushmore.
Wit: What happened?
Nit: They couldn't find rock that was thick enough.

Nit: I went to my doctor and told him I was having trouble breathing.
Wit: Really? What did he say?
Nit: He told me he could give me something to stop it.

Nit: Do you like your job cleaning chimneys?
Wit: It certainly soots me.

Nit: Is it true that pigs make good drivers?
Wit: I hear they're road hogs.

Nit: I don't like the cheese with holes in it.
Wit: Okay, just eat the cheese and leave the holes on the side of your plate.

Nit: My ancestors came over on the Mayflower.
Wit: My ancestors came over a month before—on the April Shower.

Nit: I just love to be in the country and hear the trees whisper.
Wit: That may be okay, but I hate to hear the grass mown.

2

Quirky Queries

How do you get rid of a spotted dog?
Use spot remover.

How do locomotives hear?
Through their engineers.

How do you get water into watermelons?
You plant them in the spring.

How do you keep a dog from barking in the back of the car?
Put him in the front seat.

How many controls do you have on your TV set?
Six, most of the time—my father, my mother, and my four sisters.

How do you know when an elephant is in your bed?
He has an E on his pajamas.

How can you put yourself through a keyhole?
Write "yourself" on a piece of paper and push it through.

How do you make notes of stone?
Just rearrange the letters.

How can you carry water in a sieve?
Make it into a block of ice first.

How do you make a strawberry shake?
Take it to a horror film.

How do you stop a gelatin race?
Shout, "Get set!"

How does a pig get to the hospital?
In a hambulance!

How do you keep flies out of the kitchen?
Keep your garbage can in the living room.

How did the man feel when he got his electric bill?
He was shocked.

How do you know that eating carrots is good for the eyes?
Have you ever seen a rabbit wearing eyeglasses?

Where are the largest diamonds in New York City kept?
In the baseball fields.

Where do sick ships go?
To the docs.

Where do cats like to go on vacation?
The Canary Islands.

Where does a chimney sweep keep his brushes?
In a soot case.

Where can you see man-eating plants?
In a vegetarian restaurant!

Where did Julius Caesar go on his thirty-ninth birthday?
Into his fortieth year.

Where does a golfer dance?
At the golf ball.

Where does the sandman keep his sleeping bag?
In a nap sack.

Where do tadpoles go to change into frogs?
The croakroom.

Where is the fencing master?
He's out to lunge.

Who was the biggest bandit in history?
Atlas. He held up the world.

Who brings the monster's babies?
Frankenstork.

Who has a sack and bites people?
Santa Jaws.

Who is Santa Claus's wife?
Mary Christmas.

Who dares to sit before the queen with his hat on?
Her chauffeur.

Who makes up jokes about knitting?
A nitwit.

Who is the smallest man in history?
The sailor who went to sleep on his watch.

What do you get when you cross a porcupine with a mole?
A tunnel that leaks.

What do you get when you cross a cow and a pogo stick?
A milkshake.

What do you get when you cross a worm and a fur coat?
A caterpillar.

What do you get when you cross a gangster and a garbage man?
Organized grime.

What do you get when you cross a movie house and a swimming pool?
A dive-in theater.

What do you get when you cross a clock and a chicken?
An alarm cluck.

Where does a snowflake dance?
At the snowball.

What do you get when you cross a lion and a monkey?
A swinging lion.

Why would the jailed man want to catch the measles?
So he could break out.

Why wasn't the man hurt when he jumped off the Empire State Building?
Because he was wearing his light fall suit.

Why are spiders like tops?
They are always spinning.

Why are country people smarter than city people?
The population is denser in big cities.

Why can't you keep secrets in a bank?
Because of all the tellers.

Why are sheep poor?
Because they're always getting fleeced.

Why is your sense of touch impaired when you are ill?
Because you don't feel well.

Why are fish smart?
Because they swim in schools.

Why did the little boy take an umbrella to church?
Because he heard the pastor was going to preach up a storm.

Why did the chicken cross the muddy road and not come back?
Because he didn't want to be a dirty double crosser!

Why is the letter K like a pig's tail?
Because it's the end of pork.

Why is the letter E like London?
Because it is the capital in England.

Why is going to school like taking a bath?
After you're in it a while, it's not so hot.

Why is it that when you are looking for something, you always find it in the last place you look?
Because you always stop looking when you find it.

Why is it so hard to fool a snake?
You can't pull his leg.

Why are talkative people and male pigs alike?
Because after a while both of them become bores.

Why should the number 288 never be mentioned in polite company?
Because it is two gross.

When does a boat show affection?
When it hugs the shore.

When is a piece of wood like a queen?
When it is made into a ruler.

When does a leopard change his spots?
When he moves.

When are cooks most cruel?
When they beat the eggs and whip the cream.

When was beef the highest it has ever been?
When the cow jumped over the moon.

Why shouldn't you cry when a cow slips and falls on the ice?
Because it's no use crying over spilt milk.

When you take away two letters from this five-letter word, you are left with one. What's the word?
Stone.

When is an eye not an eye?
When an onion makes it water.

When does a mouse weigh as much as an elephant?
When the scale is broken.

When does a teacher wear dark glasses?
When she has bright pupils.

When does it rain money?
Whenever there's change in the weather.

When is a rope like a piece of wood?
When it has knots.

When is a gardener like a story writer?
When he works up his plot.

When is a pint of milk not a pint?
When it's condensed.

When is a cigar like dried beef?
When it is smoked.

When is a man not a man?
When he turns into an alley.

When is an airplane not an airplane?
When it's aloft.

When do you have four hands?
When you double your fists.

When is a boy not a boy?
When he's a little hoarse.

When is a blow on the head like a piece of fabric?
When it is felt.

When is a frog unable to talk?
When he's got a man in his throat.

When does the captain of a yacht get a traffic ticket for careless piloting?
When he sails past a red lighthouse.

When is a sailor not a sailor?
When he's aboard.

When does a public speaker steal lumber?
When he takes the floor.

When can a giant be small?
When he's with his big brother.

When is a store like a boat?
When it has sales.

How do you know that peanuts are fattening?
Because you never see a skinny elephant!

How do you go on a Chinese diet?
Use one chopstick.

How do we know that mountain goats have feet?
Because they are sure-footed.

How did the chimpanzee get out of his cage?
He used a monkey wrench.

How do you get a horse out of a bathtub?
Pull out the plug.

How many insects does it take to make a landlord?
Ten ants.

How does a hot coffee pot feel?
Perky.

How did the man describe his work in the towel factory?
Very absorbing.

How many skunks does it take to smell up the neighborhood?
Just a phew.

How do you prevent seasickness?
Bolt your food down.

How did the wood shaving fly from the board?
It took off on a plane.

How do you make an apple turnover?
Tickle it in the ribs.

How can you find a lost rabbit?
Make a noise like a carrot.

How can you divide 16 apples among 17 hungry people?
Make applesauce.

How did Hiawatha?
With thoap and water.

3

What are two of the smallest insects mentioned in the Bible?
The widow's "mites" and the "wicked flee"—Mark 12:42 and Proverbs 28:1.

Who is the smallest man mentioned in the Bible?
Some people believe that it was Zacchaeus. Others believe it was Nehemiah (Knee-high-a-miah) or Bildad, the Shuhite (Shoe-height). But in reality it was Peter the disciple. He slept on his watch.

One of the first things Cain did after he left the Garden of Eden was to take a nap. How do we know this?
Because he went to the land of Nod—Genesis 4:16.

Where is the first math problem mentioned in the Bible?
When God divided the light from the darkness—Genesis 1:4.

Where is the second math problem mentioned in the Bible?
When God told Adam and Eve to go forth and multiply—Genesis 1:28.

Who was the first person in the Bible to eat herself out of house and home?
Eve.

Who was the straightest man in the Bible?
Joseph. Pharaoh made a ruler out of him.

If Methuselah was the oldest man in the Bible (969 years of age), why did he die before his father?
His father was Enoch. Enoch never died; he walked with God—Genesis 5:24.

Who introduced the first walking stick?
Eve...when she presented Adam with a little Cain.

Why was Moses the most wicked man in the Bible?
Because he broke the Ten Commandments all at once.

Was there any money on Noah's ark?
Yes. The duck took a bill, the frog took a greenback, and the skunk took a scent.

Where in the Bible does it say that fathers should let their sons use the automobile?
In Proverbs 13:24—"He that spareth his rod hateth his son."

Who was the best financier in the Bible?
Noah. He floated his stock while the whole world was in liquidation.

Where does it talk about Honda cars in the Bible?
In Acts 1:14—"These all continued with one accord."

What prophet in the Bible was a space traveler?
Elijah. He went up in a fiery chariot—2 Kings 2:11.

What city in the Bible was named after something that you find on every modern-day car?
Tyre.

When the ark landed on Mount Ararat, was Noah the first one out?
No, he came forth out of the ark.

Which one of Noah's sons was considered a clown?
His second son. He was always a Ham.

Which came first—the chicken or the egg?
The chicken, of course. God doesn't lay any eggs.

Where was deviled ham mentioned in the Bible?
When the evil spirits entered the swine.

What man in the Bible spoke when he was a very small baby?
Job. He cursed the day he was born.

What did Noah say while he was loading all the animals on the ark?
Now I herd everything.

What was the first theatrical event in the Bible?
Eve's appearance for Adam's benefit.

4

Knock, knock.
Who's there?
A herd.
A herd who?
A herd you were home, so I came over!

Knock, knock.
Who's there?
Gillette.
Gillette who?
Gillette the cat out?

Knock, knock.
Who's there?
Celeste.
Celeste who?
Celeste time I'll ask you.

Knock, knock.
Who's there?
Alfred.
Alfred who?
Alfred the needle if you'll sew on the button.

Knock, knock.
Who's there?
Amis.
Amis who?
Amis is as good as a mile.

Knock, knock.
Who's there?
Despair.
Despair who?
Despair tire is at home.

Knock, knock.
Who's there?
Radio.
Radio who?
Radio not, here I come.

Knock, knock.
Who's there?
Doughnut.
Doughnut who?
Doughnut open until Christmas.

Knock, knock.
Who's there?
Oliver.
Oliver who?
Oliver troubles will soon be over.

Knock, knock.
Who's there?
Yule.
Yule who?
Yule come on down, you hear?

Knock, knock.
Who's there?
Osborne.
Osborne who?
Osborne in the state of Georgia.

Knock, knock.
Who's there?
Polly Warner.
Polly Warner who?
Polly Warner cracker.

Knock, knock.
Who's there?
Sherwood.
Sherwood who?
Sherwood like for you to let me in.

Knock, knock.
Who's there?
Howard.
Howard who?
Howard you today?

Knock, knock.
Who's there?
Phillip.
Phillip who?
Phillip the tub so I can take a bath.

Knock, knock.
Who's there?
Nixon.
Nixon who?
Nixon stones will break my bones.

Knock, knock.
Who's there?
Sarah.
Sarah who?
Sarah doctor in the house?

Knock, knock.
Who's there?
Howie.
Howie who?
Fine, thanks. Howie you?

Knock, knock.
Who's there?
Pecan.
Pecan who?
Pecan somebody your own size.

Knock, knock.
Who's there?
Omega.
Omega who?
Omega better jokes than these, please!

Knock, knock.
Who's there?
Just a minute and I'll see.

Knock, knock.
Who's there?
Yul.
Yul who?
Yul never know.

Knock, knock.
Who's there?
You.
You who?
Did you call me?

Knock, knock.
Who's there?
Hiram.
Hiram who?
Hiram fine. How are you?

Knock, knock.
Who's there?
Warrior.
Warrior who?
Warrior been all my life?

Knock, knock.
Who's there?
Oscar.
Oscar who?
Oscar silly question, get a silly answer!

Knock, knock.
Who's there?
Manuel.
Manuel who?
Manuel be sorry if you don't unlock the door!

Knock, knock.
Who's there?
Arthur.
Arthur who?
Arthur any jobs available?

Knock, knock.
Who's there?
Annie.
Annie who?
Annie body home?

Knock, knock.
Who's there?
Wooden shoe.
Wooden shoe who?
Wooden shoe like to know!

Knock, knock.
Who's there?
Noah.
Noah who?
Noah good knock–knock joke?

Knock, knock.
Who's there?
Catsup.
Catsup who?
Catsup a tree. Quick, call the fire department!

Knock, knock.
Who's there?
Huron.
Huron who?
Huron time for once.

Knock, knock.
Who's there?
Foreign.
Foreign who?
Foreign 20 blackbirds baked in a pie.

Knock, knock.
Who's there?
Cain.
Cain who?
Cain you hear me going knock, knock?

Knock, knock.
Who's there?
Bee Hive.
Bee Hive who?
Bee Hive yourself or you will get into trouble.

Knock, knock.
Who's there?
Mack.
Mack who?
Mack up your mind.

Knock, knock.
Who's there?
Pasteur.
Pasteur who?
It's Pasteur bedtime.

Knock, knock.
Who's there?
Wash Out.
Wash Out who?
Wash Out, I'm coming in!

Knock, knock.
Who's there?
Hosea.
Hosea who?
Hosea can you see?

Knock, knock.
Who's there?
Milt.
Milt who?
Milt the cow.

Knock, knock.
Who's there?
Manila.
Manila who?
Manila ice cream!

Knock, knock.
Who's there?
Easter.
Easter who?
Easter anybody home?

Knock, knock.
Who's there?
Luke.
Luke who?
Luke both ways before crossing.

Knock, knock.
Who's there?
Carrie.
Carrie who?
Carrie me inside, I'm tired.

Knock, knock.
Who's there?
Kent.
Kent who?
Kent you guess?

Knock, knock.
Who's there?
Dill.
Dill who?
Big Dill!

Knock, knock.
Who's there?
Archer.
Archer who?
Archer glad to see me?

Knock, knock.
Who's there?
Cologne.
Cologne who?
Cologne Ranger!

Knock, knock.
Who's there?
Yukon.
Yukon who?
Yukon too many people!

Knock, knock.
Who's there?
Amnesia.
Amnesia who?
Oh, I see you have it, too!

Knock, knock.
Who's there?
Canoe.
Canoe who?
Canoe please get off my foot?

Knock, knock.
Who's there?
Tuna.
Tuna who?
Tuna to a rap station!

Knock, knock.
Who's there?
Sarah.
Sarah who?
Sarah echo in here?

Knock, knock.
Who's there?
Saul.
Saul who?
Saul in your head!

Knock, knock.
Who's there?
Lotto.
Lotto who?
Lotto good that will do.

Knock, knock.
Who's there?
Mayonnaise.
Mayonnaise who?
Mayonnaise have seen the glory of the coming of the Lord...

Knock, knock.
Who's there?
Vera.
Vera who?
Vera interesting.

Knock, knock.
Who's there?
Justin.
Justin who?
Justin time for dinner.

Knock, knock.
Who's there?
Albie.
Albie who?
Albie down to get you in a taxi, honey.

Knock, knock.
Who's there?
Arch.
Arch who?
Gesundheit!

Knock, knock.
Who's there?
Abe Lincoln.
Abe Lincoln who?
Don't you know who Abe Lincoln is?

Knock, knock.
Who's there?
Alex.
Alex who?
Alex in Wonderland!

Knock, knock.
Who's there?
Uriah.
Uriah who?
Keep Uriah on the ball.

Knock, knock.
Who's there?
Ice cream.
Ice cream who?
Ice cream 'cause I'm a cheerleader.

Knock, knock.
Who's there?
Zing.
Zing who?
Zing a song of blackbirds.

Knock, knock.
Who's there?
Gladys.
Gladys who?
Gladys summer.

Knock, knock.
Who's there?
Hugh.
Hugh who?
Hugh better watch out, you better not cry…

Knock, knock.
Who's there?
Isadore.
Isadore who?
Isadore locked?

Knock, knock.
Who's there?
Luke.
Luke who?
Luke through the keyhole and see.

5

Bill: What can be right but never wrong?
Jill: I have no clue.
Bill: An angle.

Bill: What has eight legs, two arms, three heads, and wings?
Jill: I don't know.
Bill: A man on horseback with a hawk on his hand.

Bill: Please give me a ticket to the moon.
Jill: Sorry, the moon is full now.

Bill: What goes "Clomp, clomp, clomp, squish, clomp, clomp, clomp, swish"?
Jill: I can't guess.
Bill: An elephant with one wet tennis shoe.

Bill: What goes over hill and vale, makes a noise but never leaves a trail?
Jill: I have no idea.
Bill: The wind.

Bill: What dance did the Pilgrims do?
Jill: You tell me.
Bill: The Plymouth Rock.

Bill: What is a needy musician's fund called?
Jill: I give up.
Bill: A band aid.

Bill: What is in the sea and on your arm?
Jill: Who knows.
Bill: A muscle (mussel).

Bill: What did the baker do when he ran out of strawberries?
Jill: You've got me.
Bill: Made strawberry shortcake.

Bill: What do you call a grandfather clock?
Jill: My mind's a blank.
Bill: An old timer.

Bill: What do you call a cotton-eating insect that rides a motorcycle?
Jill: That's a mystery.
Bill: Weevil Knievel!

Bill: What's an organ grinder's favorite tempo?
Jill: I'm blank.
Bill: Throw-quarter time!

Bill: What is a bacteria?
Jill: I don't have the foggiest.
Bill: The rear entrance of a cafeteria.

Bill: What ant lives in a house?
Jill: It's unknown to me.
Bill: Occupant.

Bill: What can you add to a bucket of water that makes it weigh less?
Jill: I'm in the dark.
Bill: Holes.

Bill: What is everyone in the world doing at the same time?
Jill: I pass.
Bill: Getting older.

Bill: What is a sure way to grow fat?
Jill: How should I know?
Bill: Raise hogs.

Bill: What should you do if you always get sick the night before a trip?
Jill: I don't know.
Bill: Start a day earlier.

Bill: What is the first thing ghosts do when they get into a car?
Jill: I have no clue.
Bill: They boo-ckle up.

Bill: What is the best way to introduce a hamburger?
Jill: I have no clue.
Bill: Meat Patty.

Bill: What does the Lone Ranger's horse eat with?
Jill: Beats me.
Bill: Silverware.

Bill: What does a pheasant say when it kisses its children good night?
Jill: I can't guess.
Bill: Pheasant dreams.

Bill: What would you get if you crossed an almond and a briefcase?
Jill: I have no idea.
Bill: A nut case.

Bill: What did one earthquake say to the other earthquake?
Jill: You tell me.
Bill: It's all your fault.

Bill: What do you get if you cross a peacock with an insect?
Jill: I give up.
Bill: A cocky roach.

Bill: What's the best kind of trousers for a wise guy to wear?
Jill: Who knows?
Bill: Smarty-pants.

Bill: What do you call a contented rabbit?
Jill: You've got me.
Bill: Hoppy-go-lucky.

Bill: What happens if you swallow a frog?
Jill: My mind is blank.
Bill: You'll probably croak any minute.

Bill: What did Humpty Dumpty die of?
Jill: I have no clue.
Bill: Shell shock.

Bill: What's the difference between a knight in shining armor and Rudolph the Red-Nosed Reindeer?
Jill: Beats me.
Bill: One is a dragon slayer, and the other is a sleigh dragger.

Bill: What happened to the guy who stole 1,000 Three Musketeer candy bars?
Jill: I can't guess.
Bill: He ended up behind bars.

Bill: How did one cactus compliment another cactus?
Jill: I have no idea.
Bill: You look sharp today.

Bill: What did one garbage can say to the other garbage can?
Jill: You tell me.
Bill: Nothing. Garbage cans can't talk.

Bill: What do you call a Texan who moves to Alaska?
Jill: I give up.
Bill: A traitor.

Bill: What happened when the skunk wrote a novel?
Jill: Who knows?
Bill: It became a best-smeller.

Bill: What is the favorite kind of cake for police?
Jill: You've got me.
Bill: Copcakes.

Bill: What is black and white and yellow?
Jill: My mind is blank.
Bill: A bus full of zebras.

Bill: What restaurants do snails avoid?
Jill: That's a mystery.
Bill: Fast-food places.

Bill: Jill, your hands are very dirty. What would you say if I came to your house with dirty hands?
Jill: I'd be too polite to mention it.

Bill: Jill! What is this fly doing in the alphabet soup you gave me?
Jill: Learning to read.

Bill: This goulash is terrible.
Jill: That's funny. I put a brand-new pair of goulashes in it.

Bill: You mean to tell me that you've lived in this out-of-the-way town for more than 25 years? I can't see what there is here to keep you busy.
Jill: There isn't anything to keep me busy. That's why I like it!

Bill: I have eight eyes, four legs, six eyebrows, webbed fingers, and my purple hair stands straight up. What am I?
Jill: Something very ugly.

Bill: My dog has no nose. How does he smell?
Jill: Who knows?
Bill: Awful.

Bill: If you were in line at a train ticket window and the man in front of you was going to Los Angeles and the lady in back of you was going to Florida, where would you be going?
Jill: You've got me.
Bill: If you don't know, then what are you doing in line?

Bill: Can you tell me where hippos are found?
Jill: Hippos are so big that they hardly ever get lost.

Bill: Imagine meeting you here at the psychiatrist's office! Are you coming or going?

Jill: If I knew that, I wouldn't be here!

Bill: I'll bet my name is harder than yours.

Jill: All right, what's your name?

Bill: Stone.

Jill: You lose. My name is Harder.

Bill: Why did the elephant paint his toes white?

Jill: I have no clue.

Bill: So he could hide in a bag of marshmallows.

Bill: Why did the clock have to go to the mental hospital?

Jill: Beats me.

Bill: It was a little cuckoo.

Bill: Why do pickles laugh when you touch them?

Jill: I can't guess.

Bill: They're pickle-ish.

Bill: Why is a vacuum cleaner like a gossip?

Jill: I have no idea.

Bill: Because it picks up lots of dirt.

Bill: Why isn't the elderly female mayor getting reelected?

Jill: You tell me.

Bill: Because the old gray mayor just ain't what she used to be…

Bill: Why did the nutty kid put his head on the grindstone?
Jill: I give up.
Bill: To sharpen his wits.

Bill: Want to know why I stopped going to the masseur?
Jill: Sure, tell me.
Bill: He rubbed me the wrong way.

Bill: Why is it so easy to find a lost elephant?
Jill: You've got me.
Bill: It has the odor of peanuts on its breath.

Bill: Why do carpenters and plumbers write on sandpaper?
Jill: My mind is blank.
Bill: They like to give rough estimates.

Bill: Why does a hippopotamus wear glasses?
Jill: That's a mystery.
Bill: So he can read fine print.

Bill: Why did the optometrist and his wife have an argument?
Jill: I don't know.
Bill: They couldn't see eye to eye.

6

Ryan: What is black and white and has 16 wheels?
Reginald: I don't know.
Ryan: A zebra on roller skates.

Ryan: What's the difference between an orphan, a bald head, a monkey's mother, and a king's son?
Reginald: Beats me.
Ryan: An orphan has nary a parent, a bald head has no hair apparent, a mother ape is a hairy parent, and a prince is an heir apparent.

Ryan: What did the electric plug say to the wall?
Reginald: I can't guess.
Ryan: Socket to me!

Ryan: What is the difference between the rising and the setting sun?
Reginald: I have no idea.
Ryan: All the difference in the world.

Ryan: What is the difference between a hill and a pill?
Reginald: You tell me.
Ryan: One is hard to get up, while the other is hard to get down.

Ryan: What tree is always very sad?
Reginald: I give up.
Ryan: Weeping willow.

Ryan: What is it that everybody wants, yet wants to get rid of as soon as possible?
Reginald: Who knows.
Ryan: A good appetite.

Ryan: What country has a good appetite?
Reginald: You've got me.
Ryan: Hungary.

Ryan: What is the difference between a bee and a donkey?
Reginald: My mind's a blank.
Ryan: One gets all the honey, and the other gets all the whacks (wax).

Ryan: What is green, has a trunk, and hangs on a tree?
Reginald: That's a mystery.
Ryan: An unripened elephant.

Ryan: What are Arctic cows called?
Reginald: I'm blank.
Ryan: Eskimoos.

Ryan: What vegetable hurts when you step on it?
Reginald: I don't have the foggiest.
Ryan: Corn.

Ryan: What three letters turn a girl into a woman?
Reginald: It's unknown to me.
Ryan: A-G-E.

Ryan: What is white outside, green inside, and hops?
Reginald: I'm in the dark.
Ryan: A frog sandwich.

Ryan: What keeps the moon in place?
Reginald: Search me.
Ryan: Its beams.

Ryan: What bird is always in low spirits?
Reginald: You've got me guessing.
Ryan: A bluebird.

Ryan: What is the highest pleasure you can think of?
Reginald: I pass.
Ryan: Riding an airplane.

Ryan: What kind of boat is like a knife?
Reginald: How should I know?
Ryan: A cutter.

Ryan: What is the most difficult key to turn?
Reginald: I don't know.
Ryan: A donkey.

Ryan: What do you sell?
Reginald: Salt.
Ryan: I'm a salt seller, too.
Reginald: Shake.

Ryan: What does an egg get when it does too much work?
Reginald: Beats me.
Ryan: Eggshausted.

Ryan: What do you get if you cross a hippopotamus with a cat?
Reginald: I can't guess.
Ryan: A hippopotamus with nine lives.

Ryan: What belongs to you and yet is used by other people more often than by yourself?
Reginald: I have no idea.
Ryan: Your name.

Ryan: What kind of vehicles do hitchhikers like to ride in?
Reginald: You tell me.
Ryan: Pickup trucks.

Ryan: What happens when you stand behind a car?
Reginald: I give up.
Ryan: You get exhausted.

Ryan: What city are you in when you drop your waffle in the sand?
Reginald: Who knows?
Ryan: Sandy Eggo.

Ryan: What do you call a little bird at the stereo shop?
Reginald: You've got me.
Ryan: A tweeter.

Ryan: What do you call it when your brother has a brainstorm?
Reginald: My mind is blank.
Ryan: Drizzle.

Ryan: What do surgeons charge their patients?
Reginald: That's a mystery.
Ryan: Cut rates.

Ryan: What did one closet say to the other closet?
Reginald: I have no clue.
Ryan: Clothes the door.

Ryan: What animal eats the least?
Reginald: Beats me.
Ryan: The moth. It just eats holes.

Ryan: What do you call a hen that cracks jokes?
Reginald: I can't guess.
Ryan: A comedihen.

Ryan: What do you say to a liar at the dinner table?
Reginald: I have no idea.
Ryan: Pass the baloney.

Ryan: What did one needle say to another needle?
Reginald: You tell me.
Ryan: Sew tell me, what's new?

Ryan: What did the astronauts say when they found bones on the moon?
Reginald: I give up.
Ryan: I guess the cow didn't make it.

Ryan: What does an odd fellow do when he tries to get revenge?
Reginald: Who knows?
Ryan: He tries to get even.

Ryan: What do you get if you cross a potato with a beet?
Reginald: You've got me.
Ryan: A potato with bloodshot eyes.

Ryan: What happened to the guy who picked a fight at the shopping center?
Reginald: My mind is blank.
Ryan: He was malled.

Ryan: What would you get if you crossed some pasta with a boa constrictor?
Reginald: That's a mystery.
Ryan: Spaghetti that winds itself around your fork.

Ryan: What part of the Bible do people who love math read?
Reginald: I don't know.
Ryan: The book of Numbers.

Ryan: What's the difference between an elephant and a flea?
Reginald: I have no clue.
Ryan: An elephant can have fleas, but a flea can never have elephants.

Ryan: What asks no questions but receives lots of answers?
Reginald: I don't know.
Ryan: A telephone.

Ryan: What is the surest way to keep water from coming into your house?
Reginald: Beats me.
Ryan: Don't pay your water bill.

Ryan: What is the best name for the wife of an astronomer?
Reginald: I have no idea.
Ryan: Stella.

Ryan: What do you call a man who doesn't have all his fingers on one hand?
Reginald: You tell me.
Ryan: Perfectly normal, for his fingers are evenly divided between his two hands.

Ryan: What is a cheerleader's favorite drink?
Reginald: I give up.
Ryan: Root beer.

Ryan: What do you keep after giving it to someone?
Reginald: Who knows?
Ryan: A promise.

Ryan: What is the difference between an old ten dollar bill and a new one?
Reginald: You've got me.
Ryan: Nine dollars.

Ryan: What happens when you feed lemons to a cat?
Reginald: My mind is blank.
Ryan: You get a sour puss.

Ryan: What would you call a leopard that never takes a bath?
Reginald: It's unknown to me.
Ryan: The Stink Panther!

Ryan: What's black and white, white and black, and green?
Reginald: I'm blank.
Ryan: Two skunks fighting over a pickle.

Ryan: When did the pig give his girlfriend a box of candy?
Reginald: I'm in the dark.
Ryan: It was Valenswine's Day!

Ryan: What do you get when you cross a computer with an elephant?
Reginald: Search me.
Ryan: A computer with extra memory!

Ryan: What dog stands the best chance of winning the heavyweight title?
Reginald: You've got me guessing.
Ryan: A boxer, of course!

Ryan: What follows a cat wherever he goes?
Reginald: I pass.
Ryan: His tail.

Ryan: What cowboy hero fought crabgrass throughout the West?
Reginald: How should I know?
Ryan: The Lawn Ranger!

Ryan: What is Santa's favorite Easter candy?
Reginald: I don't know.
Ryan: Jolly beans!

Ryan: What is green and bumpy and leaps over buildings in a single bound?
Reginald: I have no idea.
Ryan: Super Pickle!

7

Father: Congratulations! You talked on the phone for only 45 minutes instead of the usual two hours! What happened?
Daughter: Well, it was the wrong number.

Suzie: Mummy, why does it rain?
Mother: To make things grow. To give us apples, pears, corn, and flowers.
Suzie: Then why does it rain on the pavement?

Kyle: I told my mirror a joke yesterday.
Nathan: What happened?
Kyle: It cracked up.

Customer: Are you supposed to tip the waiters around here?
Waiter: Well, yes, sir.
Customer: Then how about tipping me? I've been waiting for two hours.

Ted: Where does a 680-pound gorilla sleep?
Ned: Where?
Ted: Wherever he wants to!

Tex: Did you hear about the barn that turned to stone?
Rex: No, what happened?
Tex: The wind blew so hard it made the barn rock.

Mother: Were you a good little boy at kindergarten today?
Son: Yes, you can't get into much trouble standing in the corner all day.

Teacher: Give me a sentence using the word "politics."
Student: A parrot named Polly swallowed a watch, and now Polly ticks.

Junior: Dad, I can't find my baseball mitt.
Dad: Look in the car.
Junior: I did, but I couldn't find it.
Dad: Did you try the glove compartment?

Basketball player: We're going to win this game!
Basketball coach: I certainly hoop so.

Teacher: I wish you would stop whistling while you are studying.
Student: I'm not studying.

Hotel clerk: Please wipe the mud off your shoes when you come into this establishment.
Clyde: What shoes?

Mack: I left my watch upstairs.
Jack: Don't worry—it will run down.

Teacher: What was your mother's name before she was married?
Student: I think it must have been Hilton. That's the name on our towels.

Billy: I make money with my drums.
Willy: Oh, you play with a band?
Billy: Nope, my pop gives me a dollar a week not to play them.

Red: My dog knows math.
Fred: Really?
Red: Yes. I ask him what 27 minus 27 is, and he says nothing.

Molly: My cat can say his own name.
Marcy: What is your cat's name?
Molly: Meow.

Little leaguer: Dad, what does a ballplayer do when his eyesight starts going bad?
Dad: He gets a job as an umpire.

Magician: I can turn a handkerchief into a bouquet of flowers.
Boy: That's nothing. I can go to the corner and turn into a drugstore.

Moe: I'm going to sneeze.
Joe: At who?
Moe: At-choo!

Boy: Darling, I could die for your sake.
Girl: You are always saying that, but you never do it.

Bertram: I have a really good radio. I can get Boston, Denver, and San Francisco on it.
Clyde: That's nothing. I can stick my head out the window and get chilly.

Jonas: I can lift a shark with one hand.
Bert: I don't believe you.
Jonas: Get me a shark with one hand, and I'll show you.

City man: Is your water supply healthy?
Farmer: Yes, we use well water.

Ted: Once there was a king. In front of him were three glasses. Two were full, one wasn't. Who was he?
Ned: Beats me.
Ted: Phillip the Third.

Dora: What's red and dingle-dangles?
Debby: I don't know.
Dora: A red dingle-dangle. What's green and dingle-dangles?
Debby: A green dingle-dangle?
Dora: No, they only come in red.

Horace: Did I ever tell you about the time I was face-to-face with a lion?

Harold: No. What happened?

Horace: There I stood without a gun. The lion moved closer and closer. He was growling. He was right on top of me.

Harold: Gosh! What did you do then?

Horace: I moved on to the next cage.

Courtney: I'm putting in a claim on my medical insurance for this bump on my head.

Cora: I see. You're hoping they'll settle for a lump sum, right?

Salesperson: This new computer will do half of your company's work.

Boss: Good. I'll take two of them!

Mother: If you eat more cake, you'll burst.

Son: Well, pass the cake and get out of the way.

Lloyd: Have you ever seen a man-eating fish?

Edgar: Sure.

Lloyd: Where?

Edgar: In a seafood restaurant.

Albert: What is the best way to teach a girl to swim?

Andy: Well, you take her arm and gently let her down in the water, put your arm around her waist, and…

Albert: Cut it out. It's my sister.

Andy: Oh, push her off the dock.

First neighbor: How is your daughter getting along in her bookkeeping class at school?
Second neighbor: Terrific! Now instead of asking for her allowance, she just bills us for it.

An airplane and a helicopter went fishing.
Airplane: I'll get the fishing poles. You get the bait.
Helicopter: Why do I have to get the bait?
Airplane: Everybody knows the whirlybird gets the worm.

Rex: Why did they put the acrobat in the sanatorium?
Tex: Because he flipped out.

Angry man: Little boy, have you seen who broke my window?
Little boy: No, but have you seen my soccer ball?

Husband: Honey, this lettuce tastes funny.
Wife: It shouldn't. It's clean. I even washed it with soap.

Do you know why Robin Hood robbed only the rich?
Poor people don't have any money.

Paul: If you had only one match and entered a room in which there was a kerosene lamp, an oil heater, and a wood-burning stove, which would you light first?
Saul: The stove?
Paul: No, you'd have to light the match first.

The Englishman sat calmly in his garden and watched a flying saucer land. The creature that emerged had three eyes—one orange, one yellow, one green—and fangs. It walked on its elbows, and its nose lit up like a light bulb.

"Take me to your leader!" it commanded.

"Nonsense," said the Englishman, stirring his tea. "What you need is a plastic surgeon."

Nick: Do you mean to tell me you fell over 50 feet and didn't get a scratch?

Rick: Sure! I was just trying to get to the back of the bus.

Farmer: This is a dogwood tree.

Tourist: How can you tell?

Farmer: By its bark.

Upscale store owner: What a sweet child! Here's a treat just for you.

Upscale mother: What do you say to the nice lady?

Upscale tot: Charge it, please!

My girlfriend's so conceited, she goes to the garden to let the flowers smell her.

Sir Cecil: After my ship went down, I survived a week in the open sea on just a can of sardines.

Lady Alice: Goodness, however did you keep from falling off?

Jane: I had the radio on last night.

June: Really? How did it fit?

Eskimo boy: I'd push my dog team through a thousand miles of ice and snow to tell you that I love you.
Eskimo girl: That's a lot of mush!

Sammy had just completed his first day at school.
Mother: Well, what did you learn today?
Sammy: Not enough. I have to go back tomorrow.

Son: Is a ton of coal very much, Papa?
Papa: That depends, my son, on whether you are shoveling it or buying it.

Grandpa: When I was your age, I could name all the states and their capitals.
Grandson: Yeah, but there were only 13 states then.

Summer camp is educational. Last year I learned how to say "Help!" underwater.

I have a friend who got a job in a drugstore. But he was fired the first day after he told his boss he couldn't get the pill bottles in the typewriter.

Customer: How much are these oranges?
Grocer: Two for a quarter.
Customer: How much is just one?
Grocer: Fifteen cents.
Customer: Then I'll take the other one.

8

Did you hear about the worm that joined the army?
He's in the apple corps.

Did you hear the one about the canyon?
It's grand!

Did you hear about the football player who was injured?
The coach gave him the ball and told him to run around his own end.

Did you hear the one about the soap cleaner?
It's really clean.

Did you hear the one about the toothache?
It's a pain!

Did you hear the one about the terrible twin boys?
It's too bad!

Did you hear the one about the sewing machine?
It'll leave you in stitches!

Did you hear about the dumb crook?
He thought the easiest way to get some fast dough was to rob bakeries.

Did you hear about the patient with a split personality?
He was so stuck up he wouldn't even speak to himself.

Did you hear the joke about the lunch meat?
It's a lot of baloney.

Did you hear the joke about the bed?
It hasn't been made up yet.

Did you hear the joke about the knife?
It's a cut-up.

Did you hear the one about the boxer?
It'll knock you out!

Did you hear the one about the rocket?
It's out of sight.

Did you hear the one about the jungle?
It's wild!

Did you hear about the train engine that went crazy?
It was a loco-motive!

Did you ever hear the story about the two holes in the ground?
Well, well.

Did you hear about the newlyweds who were really skinny?
On their wedding day the guests didn't throw rice, they threw vitamins.

Did you hear the one about the salt mine?
It's pretty deep!

Did you hear about the newlyweds who were very frail?
They got knocked cold when their friends threw rice at them.

Did you hear about the kangaroo that has no pep at the San Diego Zoo?
The vet diagnosed him as out of bounds.

Did you hear about the guy who put Band-Aids in the refrigerator?
He wanted to have cold cuts.

Did you hear about the baby sardine who was afraid of the submarine?
His mother explained it was just a can full of people.

Did you hear about the absentminded train conductor?
He lost track of things.

Did you hear about the deck chair factories that lost money?
They folded.

Did you hear about the sword swallower who worked for nothing?
He was a free-lancer.

Did you hear about the absentminded musician?
He had to leave himself notes.

Did you hear about the cowboy who fell in the leaves?
He was accused of rustling.

Did you hear the joke about the mountain climber?
He hasn't made it up yet.

Did you hear about the weatherman who went back to college?
He got several degrees.

Did you hear about the weatherman who won the race?
He said it was a breeze.

Did you hear about the glue truck that overturned?
Police were asking motorists to stick to their own lanes.

Did you hear about the investigator who joined the army?
He was a private eye.

Did you hear about the accident at the string bean factory?
Two workers got canned.

Did you hear about the sewing needle that told jokes?
It could keep you in stitches.

Did you ever see a salad bowl?

Did you ever see a home run?

Did you ever see a king fish?

Did you ever see a fire fly?

Did you ever see a ginger snap?

Did you ever see a picket fence?

Did you ever see a square dance?

Did you ever see a shoe box?

Did you ever see a hot dog stand?

Did you ever see a ball park?

Did you ever see a hog bristle?

Did you ever see a stone step?

9

Why shouldn't you have a short walking stick?
Because it can never be-long to you.

Why are hogs like trees?
Because they root for a living.

Why would you iron a four-leaf clover?
To press your luck!

Why did the invisible man look in the mirror?
To see if he still wasn't there.

Why do you say that whales talk a lot?
Because they are always spouting off.

Why is a horse the most unusual eater of all animals?
Because he eats best when there isn't a bit in his mouth.

Why is the grass dangerous?
It's full of blades.

Why are all the western prairies so flat?
Because the sun sets on them every evening.

Why is your hand like a hardware store?
Because it carries nails.

Why is an eye doctor like a teacher?
They both test the pupils.

Why do gardeners hate weeds?
Give weeds an inch and they'll take a yard.

Why do frogs have it made?
Because they eat what bugs them!

Why shouldn't you tell a pig a secret?
Because he is a squealer.

Why can't a shoe talk?
Because it's tongue-tied.

Why are the boy's pants always too short?
Because feet are always sticking out.

Why is a television set like a railroad crossing?
Because it makes people stop, look, and listen.

Why was the pony called a hot-head?
Because he had a blaze on his forehead.

Why is a banana peel like a sweater?
Because you can slip on both.

Why does a hummingbird hum?
He doesn't know the words.

How did the weirdo get rid of the dalmatian?
He used spot remover!

How did Jonah feel when the whale swallowed him?
Down in the mouth.

How does a schizophrenic change a light bulb?
He asks one of his personalities to do it for him!

How did the turtle keep three jumps ahead of the rabbit?
He played checkers with him.

How do you know that robbers are strong?
They hold up banks, don't they?

Is it safe to write a letter on an empty stomach?
It is safe enough, but it is better to write the letter on paper.

A man spent a week in the mountains. He left on Friday and came back on the same Friday. How did he do it?
His donkey was named Friday.

One day two fathers and two sons went fishing. Each caught a fish. But only three fish were caught. Why is that?
Because there were only three fishermen—a boy, his father, and his grandfather.

A farmer has 3-1/3 haystacks on the east side of his property. He also has 7-3/8 haystacks on the west side of his farm. When he puts all the haystacks together how many haystacks will he have?
One.

A woman had seven children and half of them were boys. How could that be?
The other half were boys too.

A nickel and a dime were crossing a bridge, and the nickel fell off. Why didn't the dime fall too?
Because it had more cents than the nickel.

How can you make a slow horse fast?
Tie him up.

How do you make gold stew?
Add 14 carrots.

How did the rocket lose its job?
It got fired.

How can you tell a spring chicken?
By the bounce in its step.

How do computers know what to eat?
They read the menu!

How can you keep a fish from smelling?
Stick a Band-Aid across his nose.

How did the bears keep Goldilocks from reentering their house?
They put a Goldi-lock on the door!

How does a pilot cook his meals?
In a flying pan.

How many letters are there in the alphabet?
Eleven: T-h-e a-l-p-h-a-b-e-t.

How does the weirdo feel about winter?
It leaves him cold!

How do you spell cat backward?
C-a-t b-a-c-k-w-a-r-d!

How do you make a turtle fast?
Don't feed him.

How do you keep food on an empty stomach?
Bolt it down.

How can you buy eggs and be sure they have no chickens in them?
Buy duck eggs.

Why did the boy sleep on the chandelier?
Because he was a light sleeper.

Why did the man bring a rope to the baseball game?
To tie up the score.

Why do you always insist on talking about the weather to your barber?
You wouldn't have me talk about anything as exciting as politics to a man who is handling a razor, would you?

Why was the basketball player holding his nose?
Someone was taking a foul shot.

Why did the baker quit making doughnuts?
He was sick of the hole business!

Why can't a bicycle stand by itself?
Because it's two tired.

Why did the boy take a ladder to the ball game?
Because the Giants were playing.

Why did the hockey player color his teeth orange?
So they'd be easier to find on the ice.

Why is a lie like a wig?
Because it is a false hood.

Why is a pig in the house like a house afire?
Because the sooner it is put out the better.

Why is Joe such a pain in the kitchen?
He whips the cream, strains the soup, and makes the beef stew.

Why don't astronauts get hungry in space?
Because they just had a launch.

Why are fishermen and shepherds not to be trusted?
Because they live by hook and by crook.

Why does Santa Claus always go down the chimney?
Because it soots him.

Why is a lawyer like a crow?
Because he likes to have his cause heard.

Why does a preacher have an easier time than a doctor or a lawyer?
Because it is easier to preach than to practice.

Why should we not believe one word that comes from Holland?
Because Holland is such a low-lying country.

Why is a bride always unlucky on her wedding day?
Because she does not marry the best man.

Why was the moron able to buy ice at half price?
Because it was melted.

Why did the elephant wear green sneakers?
His blue ones were at the laundry.

Why wouldn't mother let the doctor operate on father?
Because she didn't want anybody else to open her male.

Why is the sea measured in knots?
They keep the ocean tied.

Why do women not become bald as soon as men?
Because they wear their hair longer.

Why is it so hard to make frogs cry?
They're always hoppy.

Why does it take longer to run from second base to third base than it takes to run from first base to second base?
Because there's a shortstop between second and third.

Why is a cat like a transcontinental highway?
Because it's fur from one end to the other.

Why does your sense of touch suffer when you are ill?
Because you don't feel well.

Why does a policeman have brass buttons on his coat?
To button up his coat.

Why would a compliment from a chicken be an insult?
Because it would be fowl language.

Why do lions eat raw meat?
Because they don't know how to cook.

Why did the orange stop in the middle of the road?
Because it ran out of juice.

Why did the silly kid put an alarm clock in his shoe?
Because he didn't want his foot to fall asleep.

Why are dudes no longer imported into this country from England?
Because a Yankee-doodle-doo.

Why do people laugh up their sleeves?
Because that is where their funnybones are.

Why do peasants wear capes?
To cape them warm.

Why was the baseball player arrested in the middle of the game?
He was caught stealing second base.

Why do turkeys have small appetites?
Because they are always stuffed.

Why couldn't the mummy talk over the telephone?
Because he was all tied up.

Why was the letter so damp?
It had postage dew.

Why was the cow going to the psychiatrist?
She had a fodder complex.

Why couldn't the electric car go from coast to coast?
The extension cord was too short.

Why do some fishermen use helicopters to get their bait?
Because the whirlybird gets the worm.

Why was the photographer arrested?
Because he shot people and blew them up.

Why was Cinderella such a poor runner?
Because she had a pumpkin for a coach.

Why did George put a blindfold on?
So he could go on a blind date.

Why did the chicken run away from home?
She felt cooped up.

Why are jazz musicians sweet?
Because they play in jam sessions.

Why is a clergyman like a shoemaker?
Both try to save soles.

Why did the schoolteacher marry the janitor?
Because he swept her off her feet.

Why is a thief like a thermometer on a hot day?
Because they are both up to something.

Why shouldn't you tell a joke while you are ice skating?
Because the ice might crack up.

10

Calvin: What do electricians study in school?
Cora: I have no clue.
Calvin: Current events!

Calvin: What's worse than finding half a worm in your apple?
Cora: I don't know.
Calvin: Finding a frog in your throat.

Calvin: What kind of teeth can you buy for a dollar?
Cora: Beats me.
Calvin: Buck teeth.

Calvin: What tree can you hold in your hand?
Cora: I have no idea.
Calvin: A palm.

Calvin: What has a beard and no legs?
Cora: You tell me.
Calvin: A chin.

Calvin: What kind of gum do bees make?
Cora: I give up.
Calvin: Bumble gum.

Calvin: What dessert is appropriate for a shoemaker?
Cora: Who knows?
Calvin: Cobbler.

Calvin: What is the best name for the wife of a train conductor in charge of the sleeping cars?
Cora: You've got me.
Calvin: Bertha.

Calvin: What letter is most useful to a deaf woman?
Cora: My mind is blank.
Calvin: The letter A, because it makes her hear.

Calvin: What is the best thing to take when one is run down?
Cora: That's a mystery.
Calvin: The license number of the car.

Calvin: What happens to a man who starts home to dinner and misses his train?
Cora: I'm blank.
Calvin: He catches it when he gets home.

Calvin: What is the main reason for using a cookie sheet?
Cora: I don't have the foggiest.
Calvin: For cookies to sleep on.

Calvin: What is the difference between a well-dressed man and a tired dog?
Cora: It's unknown to me.
Calvin: The man wears an entire suit, the dog just pants.

Calvin: What three letters make a man of a boy?
Cora: I'm in the dark.
Calvin: A-G-E.

Calvin: What kind of doctor would a duck become?
Cora: You've got me guessing.
Calvin: A quack doctor.

Calvin: What is the best name for the wife of a fisherman?
Cora: I pass.
Calvin: Nettie.

Calvin: What is the difference between a new five-cent piece and an old-fashioned quarter?
Cora: I have no idea.
Calvin: Twenty cents.

Calvin: What do you say to a king who falls off his chair?
Cora: I have no clue.
Calvin: Throne for a loop?

Calvin: What did the dog say when someone grabbed his tail?
Cora: Beats me.
Calvin: That's the end of me!

Calvin: What do you call a baby who is learning to talk?
Cora: I can't guess.
Calvin: A little word processor.

Calvin: What do you do with all the fruit that grows around here?
Cora: Well, we eat what we can—and what we can't, we can!

Calvin: What did the baked potato say to the cook?
Cora: You tell me.
Calvin: Foiled again!

Calvin: What do you get if your stockings fall off, your ornaments break, and Santa tracks soot through your living room?
Cora: I give up.
Calvin: A merry Chris-mess.

Calvin: What does a king drink when he doesn't like coffee?
Cora: Who knows?
Calvin: Royal tea.

Calvin: What did the baby banana say to the mother banana?
Cora: You've got me.
Calvin: I don't peel good.

Calvin: What do you call a bear who cries a lot?
Cora: My mind is blank.
Calvin: Winnie the Boo-hoo.

Calvin: What do you call little bugs that live on the moon?
Cora: That's a mystery.
Calvin: Lunaticks.

Calvin: How does a hobo travel?
Cora: I have no clue.
Calvin: On a tramp steamer.

Calvin: How come you don't answer the door?
Cora: It never asks any questions.

Calvin: How did your horse farm turn out?
Cora: Terrible. I planted the horses too deep.

Calvin: How is the astronomer doing?
Cora: Things are looking up.

Calvin: How did the exconvict do at his job at the music store?
Cora: You tell me.
Calvin: Not too well, they found out he had a record.

Calvin: How do bees get to school?
Cora: I give up.
Calvin: They wait at the buzz stop.

Calvin: How did you know the frog was sick?
Cora: You've got me.
Calvin: He toad me.

Calvin: How did the comedian like his eggs?
Cora: My mind is blank.
Calvin: Funny side up.

Calvin: How do you paint a rabbit?
Cora: That's a mystery.
Calvin: With hare spray.

Calvin: What is the name of the person who brings gifts to the dentist's office?
Cora: I have no clue.
Calvin: Santa Floss.

Calvin: What do you think a Laplander is?
Cora: Beats me.
Calvin: Someone who can't keep his balance while riding on a bus.

Calvin: It's Washington's birthday, so I baked you a cherry pie.
Cora: All right, bring me a hatchet so I can cut it.

Calvin: Abraham Lincoln once dined at this very table in my house.
Cora: Is that why you haven't changed the tablecloth since?

Calvin: If a man was locked up in a room with only a bat and a piano, how could he get out?
Cora: You tell me.
Calvin: There are two ways: He could swing the bat three times for an out or use a piano key.

Calvin: My brother just opened a candy business.
Cora: Is he doing well?
Calvin: So far he's made a mint.

Calvin: I had a wrestler friend who didn't feel well so he went to the doctor.
Cora: What did the doctor say?
Calvin: He told him to get a grip on himself.

Calvin: I wrote a letter to Dear Abby. This is what I said—"Dear Abby: Is it good manners to answer a question with just a single word? Signed, Polite."
Cora: Did she write back?
Calvin: Yes. This is what she said to me—"Dear Polite: No."

Calvin: I would like to go on a boat trip, but I can't afford it.
Cora: I know. Beggars can't be cruisers.

Calvin: Do moths cry?
Cora: That's a mystery.
Calvin: Yes. Haven't you ever seen a moth bawl?

Calvin: What did the comedian say to the cattle rancher?
Cora: I have no clue.
Calvin: Herd any good ones lately?

Calvin: What did Adam say to Eve on the night of December 24?
Cora: Beats me.
Calvin: Is this Christmas, Eve?

Calvin: What game do you play with bees?
Cora: I can't guess.
Calvin: Hive and seek.

Calvin: What do they call a young rabbit that never goes outside the house?
Cora: I have no idea.
Calvin: An ingrown hare.

Calvin: How can you tell the difference between the land and the ocean?
Cora: You tell me.
Calvin: The land is dirty and the ocean is tidey.

Calvin: What entertainment did Noah hire for the animals?
Cora: I give up.
Calvin: An arkestra.

Calvin: What did Mary order when she went out for dinner?
Cora: Who knows?
Calvin: Everybody knows that Mary had a little lamb.

Calvin: What did the duck say to Jack Frost?
Cora: You've got me.
Calvin: How about a quacker, Jack?

Calvin: What do you get when you cross Moby Dick and a Timex wristwatch?
Cora: My mind is blank.
Calvin: A whale watcher.

Calvin: What did the nutty guy say when he saw a bowl of Cheerios?
Cora: That's a mystery.
Calvin: Look—doughnut seeds!

Calvin: What did the sock say to the needle?
Cora: I don't know.
Calvin: I'll be darned!

Calvin: What do you call a horse that never stops telling you what to do?
Cora: I have no clue.
Calvin: A real nag.

Calvin: What seems to be your trouble?
Cora: After I get up in the morning, I'm always dizzy for half an hour.
Calvin: Then why don't you get up half an hour later?

Calvin: What did George Washington say to his men before crossing the Delaware?
Cora: I can't guess.
Calvin: Get in the boat.

Calvin: What did the jelly bean say to the Milky Way bar?
Cora: I have no idea.
Calvin: Smile, you're on candied camera.

Calvin: What's the cure for Monday-morning blues?
Cora: You tell me.
Calvin: Tuesday.

Calvin: What kind of monkey flies?
Cora: I give up.
Calvin: A hot-air baboon.

Calvin: What do ducks eat for breakfast?
Cora: Who knows?
Calvin: Quacker Oats.

Calvin: What do you say to a crying whale?
Cora: You've got me.
Calvin: Quit your blubbering.

Calvin: What is a mosquito's favorite sport?
Cora: My mind is blank.
Calvin: Skin diving.

Calvin: What happened on the Fourth of July?
Cora: That's a mystery.
Calvin: I don't know either. I'm not good at fractions.

11

Here Come the Elephants

Why are elephants gray and wrinkled all over?
Because they are difficult to iron.

Why do elephants lie in the sun a lot?
Because no one likes a white elephant.

How do you make an elephant float?
Two scoops of ice-cream, soda, and some elephant!

How do you fit six elephants in your car?
Three in the back, three in the front!

How do you run over an elephant?
Climb up his tail, dash to his head, then slide down the trunk!

What did the elephants say when they saw the French president?
Nothing. Elephants can't speak French!

How can you catch an elephant?
Hide in the grass and make a noise like a peanut!

How can you tell when there's an elephant in your refrigerator?
You can see his footprints in the cheesecake.

Why are elephants' tusks easier to get in Alabama?
Because they're "Tuscaloosa."

Why does an elephant have a trunk?
Because he'd look pretty silly with a glove compartment.

Why do elephants' tusks stick way out?
Because their parents won't allow them to get braces!

Why do elephants have trunks?
They can't afford suitcases!

Why are elephants gray?
So you can tell them from blueberries.

Why do elephants clip their toenails?
So their ballet slippers will fit.

Why do elephants step on lily pads?
Because they can't walk on water.

How can you tell when there is an elephant in your sandwich?
When it is too heavy to lift.

What do you do when an elephant stubs his toe?
Call a toe truck.

What has an elephant's trunk, a giraffe's neck, a bird's beak, and a lion's head?
A zoo.

Why do elephants hide behind trees?
To trip the ants.

How can you tell when there is an elephant under your bed?
When you are nearly touching the ceiling.

What words do you use to scold an elephant?
Tusk! Tusk!

Why did the elephant paint her head yellow?
She wanted to see if blondes have more fun.

What did the grape say when the elephant stepped on it?
Nothing. It just let out a little whine.

What's the difference between an elephant and peanut butter?
An elephant won't stick to the roof of your mouth.

How do you get an elephant out of a Jell-O box?
Read the directions on the back.

Why did the elephant walk around in polka-dot socks?
Someone stole his sneakers.

12

Knock, knock.
Who's there?
Noah.
Noah who?
Noah good place to eat around here?

Knock, knock.
Who's there?
Anita.
Anita who?
Anita minute to think it over.

Knock, knock.
Who's there?
Fitzby.
Fitzby who?
Fitzbyginning to look a lot like Christmas…

Knock, knock.
Who's there?
Razor.
Razor who?
Razor your hands. This is a stick up.

Knock, knock.
Who's there?
Owl.
Owl who?
Owl aboard.

Knock, knock.
Who's there?
Yukon.
Yukon who?
Yukon say that again.

Knock, knock.
Who's there?
Doris.
Doris who?
Doris open. Mind if I come in?

Knock, knock.
Who's there?
Barbara.
Barbara who?
Barbara black sheep, have you any wool?

Knock, knock.
Who's there?
Owl.
Owl who?
Owl be seeing you!

Knock, knock.
Who's there?
Hugo.
Hugo who?
Hugo your way—I'll go mine!

Knock, knock.
Who's there?
Waterloo.
Waterloo who?
Waterloo doing for dinner?

Knock, knock.
Who's there?
Hollywood.
Hollywood who?
Hollywood be here if she could!

Knock, knock.
Who's there?
Whittier.
Whittier who?
Whittier people always tell knock-knock jokes!

Knock, knock.
Who's there?
John.
John who?
John your mark, get set, go!

Knock, knock.
Who's there?
Esther.
Esther who?
Esther a doctor in the house?

Knock, knock.
Who's there?
Hannah.
Hannah who?
Hannah over all your money. This is a stickup!

Knock, knock.
Who's there?
China.
China who?
China cold out, isn't it?

Knock, knock.
Who's there?
Kenya.
Kenya who?
Kenya open the door?

Knock, knock.
Who's there?
Ghana.
Ghana who?
Ghana make you laugh!

Knock, knock.
Who's there?
April.
April who?
April showers.

Knock, knock.
Who's there?
Eric.
Eric who?
Eric conditioner.

Knock, knock.
Who's there?
Witless.
Witless who?
Witless ring I thee wed.

Knock, knock.
Who's there?
Hugh Maid.
Hugh Maid who?
Hugh Maid your bed, now lie in it!

Knock, knock.
Who's there?
Tacoma.
Tacoma who?
Tacoma all this way and you don't recognize me!

Knock, knock.
Who's there?
Telly.
Telly who?
Telly scope.

Knock, knock.
Who's there?
Moth.
Moth who?
Moth grows on the north side of trees.

Knock, knock.
Who's there?
Boo.
Boo who?
Crybaby!

Knock, knock.
Who's there?
Cows go.
Cows go who?
No, cows go "moo."

Knock, knock.
Who's there?
Howell.
Howell who?
Howell I get in if you don't open the door?

Knock, knock.
Who's there?
Abbey.
Abbey who?
Abbey birthday.

Knock, knock.
Who's there?
Police.
Police who?
Police stop telling me these nutty knock-knock jokes!

Knock, knock.
Who's there?
Freeze.
Freeze who?
Freeze a jolly good fellow...

Knock, knock.
Who's there?
Henrietta.
Henrietta who?
Henrietta worm that was in his apple.

Knock, knock.
Who's there?
Annapolis.
Annapolis who?
Annapolis day keeps the doctor away.

Knock, knock.
Who's there?
Adam.
Adam who?
Adam my way, I'm coming in!

Knock, knock.
Who's there?
Kenya.
Kenya who?
Kenya hear me knocking?

Knock, knock.
Who's there?
Midas.
Midas who?
Midas well try again.

Knock, knock.
Who's there?
Watson.
Watson who?
Nothing much, Watson new with you?

Knock, knock.
Who's there?
Marsha.
Marsha who?
Marshamallow.

Knock, knock.
Who's there?
Me.
Me who?
Don't you know your name?

Knock, knock.
Who's there?
Soda lady.
Soda lady who?
Quit yodeling and let me in!

Knock, knock.
Who's there?
Canoe.
Canoe who?
Canoe come out and play?

Knock, knock.
Who's there?
Doughnut.
Doughnut who?
Doughnut bother me with silly questions!

Knock, knock.
Who's there?
Carla.
Carla who?
Carla locksmith. My key won't work.

Knock, knock.
Who's there?
Ben.
Ben who?
Ben looking all over for you.

Knock, knock.
Who's there?
Aaron.
Aaron who?
Aaron out my stinky gym locker!

Knock, knock.
Who's there?
My panther.
My panther who?
My panther falling down.

Knock, knock.
Who's there?
Hank.
Hank who?
You're welcome!

Knock, knock.
Who's there?
Annette.
Annette who?
Annette is needed to catch butterflies.

Knock, knock.
Who's there?
Pasture.
Pasture who?
Pasture bedtime, isn't it?

Knock, knock.
Who's there?
Thistle.
Thistle who?
Thistle teach you not to ask silly questions.

13

Edgar: What Jack paints people's windows?
Emily: I have no clue.
Edgar: Jack Frost.

Edgar: What animals do you find in the clouds?
Emily: I don't know.
Edgar: Rain, dear.

Edgar: What two animals go with you everywhere?
Emily: Beats me.
Edgar: Your calves.

Edgar: What is the difference between a skilled marksman and the man who tends the targets?
Emily: I can't guess.
Edgar: One hits the mark, and the other marks the hits.

Edgar: What is the difference between one yard and two yards?
Emily: I have no idea.
Edgar: Usually a fence.

Edgar: What has eyes but can't see?
Emily: You tell me.
Edgar: A potato.

Edgar: What did the judge say when a skunk walked into the courtroom?
Emily: I give up.
Edgar: Odor in the court!

Edgar: What does everyone have to catch before they can sing?
Emily: Who knows?
Edgar: Their breath.

Edgar: What's the difference between a man and a banana peel?
Emily: You've got me.
Edgar: Sometimes a man throws a banana peel in the gutter, and sometimes a banana peel throws a man in the gutter.

Edgar: What's the right kind of lumber for castles in the air?
Emily: My mind's a blank.
Edgar: Sunbeams.

Edgar: What's the longest piece of furniture in the world?
Emily: I'm blank.
Edgar: The multiplication table.

Edgar: What is Batman's favorite sport?
Emily: I don't have the foggiest.
Edgar: Batminton.

Edgar: What gadget do we use to see through a wall?
Emily: It's unknown to me.
Edgar: A window.

Edgar: What's black and white and red all over?
Emily: I'm in the dark.
Edgar: Burnt toast with margarine and ketchup.

Edgar: What starts with T, ends with T, and is full of T?
Emily: Search me.
Edgar: A teapot.

Edgar: What animal has two humps and is found at the North Pole?
Emily: You've got me guessing.
Edgar: A lost camel.

Edgar: What lurks around the bottom of the sea and makes offers you can't refuse?
Emily: I pass.
Edgar: The Codfather.

Edgar: What goes "tick, tock, croak. Tick, tock, croak"?
Emily: How should I know?
Edgar: A watch frog.

Edgar: What dessert is always served in heaven?
Emily: I have no clue.
Edgar: Angel food cake!

Edgar: What do you call a meat thief?
Emily: I don't know.
Edgar: A hamburglar.

Edgar: What happened when the boy gorilla was dumped by his girlfriend?
Emily: I can't guess.
Edgar: He went ape!

Edgar: What would you call a dinosaur who's a lousy driver?
Emily: I have no idea.
Edgar: Tyrannosaurus Wrecks!

Edgar: What is a cheerleader's favorite color?
Emily: You tell me.
Edgar: Yeller.

Edgar: What did the lunatic say to his girlfriend?
Emily: I give up.
Edgar: I'm crazy about you.

Edgar: What did the walls say to the floor?
Emily: Who knows?
Edgar: I have you surrounded.

Edgar: What do you call a happy Lassie?
Emily: You've got me.
Edgar: A jolly collie!

Edgar: Ask a question that cannot be answered with yes.
Emily: My mind is blank.
Edgar: Are you asleep?

Edgar: What is the best name for the wife of an upholsterer?
Emily: That's a mystery.
Edgar: Sophie.

Edgar: What kind of food improves your vision?
Emily: I don't have the foggiest.
Edgar: Sea food.

Edgar: What did the dog say when he sat on sandpaper?
Emily: It's unknown to me.
Edgar: Ruff! Ruff!

Edgar: What do you call a little turkey that looks in other people's windows?
Emily: I'm in the dark.
Edgar: A Peeping Tom.

Edgar: What's that you have there?
Emily: A clamp.
Edgar: Oh, so you're a vise guy.

Edgar: What do you call a nutty dog in Australia?
Emily: I pass.
Edgar: A dingo-ling!

Edgar: What's the best paper for making kites?
Emily: How should I know?
Edgar: Flypaper.

Edgar: What kind of seal does housework?
Emily: I don't know.
Edgar: The Good Housekeeping Seal.

Edgar: What's the difference between a jeweler and a jailer?
Emily: I have no idea.
Edgar: One sells watches, and one watches cells.

Edgar: What is the recipe to make a chocolate drop?
Emily: I have no clue.
Edgar: Let it fall from your hand.

Edgar: How did the police describe the hitchhiker?
Emily: Beats me.
Edgar: They gave a thumbnail description.

Edgar: How did the farmer count his cows?
Emily: I can't guess.
Edgar: He used a cowculator.

Edgar: How is the monogram business you started?
Emily: I've had some initial success.

Edgar: How did your dog get a new apartment?
Emily: You tell me.
Edgar: He signed a leash.

Edgar: What is the best way to find a math tutor?
Emily: I give up.
Edgar: Place an add.

Edgar: How much did the polar bear weigh?
Emily: Who knows?
Edgar: A tondra.

Edgar: How do you make a skeleton laugh?
Emily: You've got me.
Edgar: Tickle its funny bone.

Edgar: How do you glue your mouth shut?
Emily: My mind is blank.
Edgar: With lipstick.

Edgar: Did you like the carnival?
Emily: Oh, I don't know.
Edgar: Well, I thought it was fair.

Edgar: How can you tell when there's a mosquito in your bed?
Emily: I don't know.
Edgar: By the M on its pajamas.

Edgar: I love to cook breakfast for my friends. Is it proper for me to cook it in my pajamas?
Emily: It's not improper, but it can be a big mess. I recommend a frying pan.

Edgar: You never seem to age. I wonder if you can tell me how I could avoid getting wrinkles.
Emily: Beats me.
Edgar: Maybe I should stop sleeping in my clothes.

Edgar: Did you hear about the golfer?
Emily: No, I didn't. What about him?
Edgar: He joined a club.

Edgar: I'm studying to be a barber.
Emily: Will it take long?
Edgar: No, I'm learning all the shortcuts.

Edgar: Well, Emily, how do you like school?
Emily: Closed!

Edgar: Did you get hurt when you fell and struck the piano?
Emily: No, I hit the soft pedal.

Edgar: Will your dog eat off my hand?
Emily: Yes, and he will eat off your leg, too.

Edgar: Mississippi is a very long word, but I can spell it.
Emily: Okay, spell it.
Edgar: I-T.

Edgar: Is there any difference between lightning and electricity?
Emily: Yes. You don't have to pay for lightning.

Edgar: Did you hear about the Texas millionaire whose wife was sick?
Emily: No, what happened?
Edgar: He walked into the Cadillac salesroom and said, "My wife has a touch of the flu. Do you have anything in the way of a get-well car?"

Edgar: Why does a frog have more lives than a cat?
Emily: I have no clue.
Edgar: Because it croaks every night.

Edgar: Why did the baseball player go to the store?
Emily: Beats me.
Edgar: For a sales pitch.

Edgar: Why did the class clown give a smart girl a dog biscuit?
Emily: I can't guess.
Edgar: He heard she was the teacher's pet.

Edgar: Why did the bee go to the doctor?
Emily: I have no idea.
Edgar: It had hives.

Edgar: Why was the plumber so tired?
Emily: You tell me.
Edgar: He felt drained.

Edgar: Why did the pinky go to jail?
Emily: I give up.
Edgar: He was fingered by the police.

Edgar: Why did the bird always like to sit down?
Emily: Who knows?
Edgar: He was a stool pigeon.

Edgar: Why did the nutty boy lock his father in the refrigerator?
Emily: You've got me.
Edgar: Because he wanted a cold pop.

Edgar: Why did the turkey cross the road?
Emily: My mind is blank.
Edgar: Because the chicken retired and moved to Florida.

Edgar: Why did the cottage go on a diet?
Emily: That's a mystery.
Edgar: It wanted to be a lighthouse.

Edgar: Why are you shivering, Emily?
Emily: I guess it must be this zero on my test paper.

"My new car turned out to be a lemon," he said sourly.

"How time flies," he said weakly.

"I'll never go near another skunk again," he said distinctly.

"I'm not trying to pin you down," he said pointedly.

"I use mouthwash every morning," he said breathlessly.

"I use my camera when people aren't looking," he said candidly.

"You cut me to the quick," he said sharply.

"The lemonade needs more sugar," he complained bitterly.

"Let's go camping," he said intently.

"A crocodile sandwich, please, and make it snappy!"

15

Doc, one night I dreamed I was in a wigwam, the next night I dreamed I was living in a tepee. What's happening to me?
Nothing. You're just two tents (too tense).

Doc, what's your best suggestion for this terrible breath I have?
Lockjaw.

Doc, I can't sleep at night. What should I do?
Sleep during the day.

Doc, what do you charge for a visit?
I charge $50 for the first visit and $25 for each visit thereafter.
Well, I'm here again.
Fine, then take the same prescription I gave last time.

Patient: My doctor classified me as a workaholic and suggested I get psychiatric treatment.
Friend: So what did you do?
Patient: I got another job so I could afford a psychiatrist.

Nurse: There is a man outside with a wooden leg named Smith.
Doctor: What is the name of his other leg?

Patient: You have to help me, Doctor. My wife thinks she is a pretzel.
Doctor: Bring her in to see me. Maybe I can straighten her out.

Doctor: Ask the accident victim what his name is so we can notify his family.
Nurse: He says his family knows his name.

Patient: Doctor, if a person's brain stops working, does he die?
Doctor: How can you ask such a stupid question! You're alive, aren't you?

Patient: Doctor, do you think cranberries are healthy?
Doctor: Well, I've never heard one complain.

Doctor: Deep breathing, you understand, destroys germs.
Patient: Yes, Doctor, but how can I force them to breathe deeply?

Patient: What should I do? I have water on the knee.
Doctor: Wear pumps.

I know one patient who said to the dentist, "Doctor, I think you've pulled the wrong tooth."

The dentist looked in again and said, "No, I pulled the right tooth. You got the cavity in the wrong one." Then he added, "Look on the bright side. If this tooth ever does go bad, you won't have to have it pulled again."

Doctor: How long have you had this problem?

Patient: Two days.

Doctor: Why didn't you come see me sooner?

Patient: I did. That's how long I've been in your waiting room.

Patient: Help me, Doc. I keep making long distance calls to myself and I'm going broke!

Psychiatrist: Try reversing the charges.

Psychiatrist: Well, George, you're making great progress, which is more than I can say for Stanley in Ward J. He keeps telling everyone he's going to buy the Vatican! Can you believe that?

George: No, I can't. After all, I've told him a million times I won't sell.

Patient: Will my chicken pox be better next week, Doctor?

Doctor: I don't know I hate to make rash promises.

Patient: Doctor, doctor, I feel like a bar of soap.

Doctor: That's life, boy.

Reporter: Did you ever make a serious mistake, Doctor?

Physician: I once cured a millionaire in three visits.

Dentist: Let me know if I hurt you.
Patient: I'm going to let everybody know if you hurt me.

Patient: Doctor, my life is a mess. I just don't think I can go on this way anymore.
Psychiatrist: Yes, we all have problems. I can help you, but it'll take time. We'll start at four sessions a week. My fee is a hundred dollars an hour.
Patient: Well, that solves your problem. What about mine?

Psychiatrist: I'm afraid there's no cure for your illness.
Patient: I'd like a second opinion.
Psychiatrist: Very well, make an appointment to see me again next week.

My doctor insulted my looks last week. He told me I had a weak heart and advised me to avoid severe shocks. His prescription was to break every mirror in my house.

Patient: Doctor, I'm terrified of robins. Every time I see one, I break into a cold sweat.
Psychiatrist: Why are you frightened of robins, Mr. Smith?
Patient: Aren't most worms?

Patient: Doctor, I feel like a trash can!
Doctor: Rubbish!

Patient: Doctor, I tend to get fat in certain places. What should I do?
Doctor: Keep away from those places.

Doctor: How were those pills I prescribed to improve your memory?
Patient: I forgot to take them!

Psychiatrist: Tell me, what is your biggest worry at this stage of your treatment?
Patient: It's thinking up a way to tell you I can't pay for today's session.

Patient: I want to thank you, Doctor. The pain in my back is gone. What was it—rheumatism?
Doctor: No, your suspenders were twisted.

A man walked into a doctor's office with his suit ripped and his arms and face bleeding.
The nurse took one look at him and asked, "Have an accident?"
The man replied, "No thanks, I already had one."

Patient: Doctor, something is wrong with me. I keep thinking I'm a frog.
Doctor: How long has this been going on?
Patient: Since I was a tadpole.

Sick boy: Doctor, when I'm all better, will I be able to program a computer?
Doctor: Of course you will, young man.
Sick boy: That's great! I couldn't program one before I got sick.

Lady: Doctor, doctor, my husband thinks he's an automobile.
Psychiatrist: Well, show him into my office.
Lady: I can't. He's double-parked outside.

The doctor told me my operation was fairly routine and not at all complicated. I told him to remember that when he makes out the bill.

Patient: Doctor, you've got to help me. My neck feels like a pipe and my muscles are as tight as steel bands.
Doctor: I think you should stop taking the iron pills.

Dentist: Stop making faces and waving your arms. I haven't touched your tooth yet.
Boy: I know. But you're standing on my foot.

Patient: I feel funny, Doctor, what shall I do?
Doctor: Go on television as a comedian.

I think it's only fair that a doctor who prescribes a placebo should be paid with counterfeit money.

16

Bible Fun

Who was the first man in the Bible to know the meaning of rib roast?
Adam.

On the ark, Noah probably got milk from the cows. What did he get from the ducks?
Quackers.

What was the difference between the 10,000 soldiers of Israel and the 300 soldiers Gideon chose for battle?
9700.

Certain days in the Bible passed by more quickly than most of the days. Which days were those?
The fast days.

Matthew and Mark have something that is not found in Luke and John. What is it?
The letter A.

At what season of the year did Eve eat the fruit?
Early in the fall.

What has God never seen, Abraham Lincoln seldom saw, and today's man sees every day?
His equal—Isaiah 40:25.

Where is medicine first mentioned in the Bible?
Where the Lord gives Moses two tablets.

Where does it say in the Bible that we should not fly in airplanes?
In Matthew 28:20—"Lo, I am with you always."

What was the name of Isaiah's horse?
Is Me. Isaiah said, "Woe, is me."

How were Adam and Eve prevented from gambling?
Their pair-o-dice was taken away from them.

What do you have that Cain, Abel, and Seth never had?
Grandparents.

What simple affliction brought about the death of Samson?
Fallen arches.

How were the Egyptians paid for goods taken by the Israelites when they fled from Egypt?
The Egyptians got a check on the bank of the Red Sea.

When is high finance first mentioned in the Bible?
When Pharaoh's daughter took a little prophet from the bulrushes.

Where is tennis mentioned in the Bible?
When Joseph served in Pharaoh's court.

Where in the Bible does it suggest that men should wash dishes?
In 2 Kings 21:13—"And I will wipe Jerusalem as a man wipeth a dish, wiping it, and turning it upside down."

Paul the apostle was a great preacher and teacher and earned his living as a tentmaker. What other occupation did Paul have?
He was a baker. We know this because he went to Fill-a-pie.

When did Moses sleep with five people in one bed?
When he slept with his forefathers.

What did Adam and Eve do when they were expelled from the Garden of Eden?
They raised Cain.

17

Doreen: What is the difference between a book of fiction and the rear light of a car?
Duncan: I have no clue.
Doreen: One is a light tale, and the other is a taillight.

Doreen: What difference is there among a rooster, Uncle Sam, and an old maid?
Duncan: I don't know.
Doreen: The rooster says "Cock-a-doodle-doo," Uncle Sam says "Yankee Doodle Doo," and the old maid says "Any dude'll do."

Doreen: What is worse than finding a worm in an apple?
Duncan: Beats me.
Doreen: Finding half a worm.

Doreen: What do you call a witch that sits in the sand?
Duncan: I can't guess.
Doreen: A sandwich.

Doreen: What is the best way to make time go fast?
Duncan: I have no idea.
Doreen: Use the spur of the moment.

Doreen: What did Paul Revere say when he finished his famous ride?
Duncan: You tell me.
Doreen: "Whoa."

Doreen: What man can raise things without lifting them?
Duncan: I give up.
Doreen: A farmer.

Doreen: What's white and goes up?
Duncan: Who knows.
Doreen: A dumb snowflake.

Doreen: What would happen if a girl should swallow her teaspoon?
Duncan: That's a mystery.
Doreen: She wouldn't be able to stir.

Doreen: What's the Secret of Success?
Duncan: It's unknown to me.
Doreen: "Takes pain," said the window.

"Keep cool," said the ice.
"Drive hard," said the hammer.
"Be up to date," said the calendar.
"Never be led," said the pencil.
"Be sharp," said the knife.
"Make light around you," said the fire.
"Stick to it," said the glue.
"Be bright," said the lamp.

Doreen: What is the difference between an auction and seasickness?
Duncan: I'm in the dark.
Doreen: One is a sale of effects, and the other is the effects of a sail.

Doreen: What has never been felt, never been seen, never been heard, never existed, and still has a name?
Duncan: You've got me guessing.
Doreen: Nothing.

Doreen: What is green, noisy, and extremely dangerous?
Duncan: How should I know?
Doreen: A stampeding herd of pickles.

Doreen: Why did the kangaroo go to the psychiatrist?
Duncan: I have no clue.
Doreen: Because it was jumpy.

Doreen: Why don't elephants dance?
Duncan: Beats me.
Doreen: Nobody ever asks them.

Doreen: Why is noodle soup good for you?
Duncan: I can't guess.
Doreen: Because it's brain food.

Doreen: Why did the runner bring his barber to the Olympics?
Duncan: I have no idea.
Doreen: He wanted to shave a few seconds off his time.

Doreen: Why does it take so long to make a politician snowman?
Duncan: You tell me.
Doreen: You have to hollow out the head first.

Doreen: Why didn't the weatherman ever get tired?
Duncan: I give up.
Doreen: He always got a second wind.

Doreen: Why do chickens think cooks are mean?
Duncan: Who knows?
Doreen: They beat eggs.

Doreen: Why did the bubble gum cross the road?
Duncan: You've got me.
Doreen: It was stuck to the chicken's foot.

Doreen: Why is it hard to carry on a conversation with a goat?
Duncan: My mind is blank.
Doreen: It's always butting in.

Doreen: Why don't ducks tell jokes while they are flying?
Duncan: That's a mystery.
Doreen: Because they would quack up.

Doreen: Why did it take so long for the elephant to cross the road?
Duncan: I don't know.
Doreen: Because the chicken had trouble carrying him.

Doreen: Why does that letter bring tears to your eyes?
Duncan: Search me.
Doreen: It's written on onionskin.

Doreen: What do you say to a boomerang on its birthday?
Duncan: I have no clue.
Doreen: Many happy returns.

Doreen: What dog is the best flyer?
Duncan: Beats me.
Doreen: An Airedale.

Doreen: What starts with E and ends with E and has one letter in it?
Duncan: I have no idea.
Doreen: An envelope.

Doreen: What would happen if you fed your dog garlic and onions?
Duncan: You tell me.
Doreen: His bark would be worse than his bite.

Doreen: What do you call fear of tight chimneys?
Duncan: Who knows?
Doreen: Santa Claustrophobia.

Doreen: What's a sheep's favorite snack?
Duncan: You've got me.
Doreen: A baaloney sandwich.

Doreen: What do you call a kitten that cheats on a test?
Duncan: My mind is blank.
Doreen: A copycat.

Doreen: What creature is smarter than a talking parrot?
Duncan: That's a mystery.
Doreen: A spelling bee.

Doreen: What's the best thing to do for fallen arches?
Duncan: I don't know.
Doreen: Pick them up.

18

Carter: What are the most loyal insects?
Clara: I have no clue.
Carter: Ticks. Once they find friends, they stick to them.

Carter: What is the best way to get in touch with a fish?
Clara: I don't know.
Carter: Drop him a line.

Carter: What is the difference between a church bell and a thief?
Clara: Beats me.
Carter: One peals from the steeple, and the other steals from the people.

Carter: What do you call a man without a spade?
Clara: I can't guess.
Carter: Douglas.

Carter: What did Farmer Jake get when he crossed a pig with a Christmas tree?
Clara: I have no idea.
Carter: A porky pine.

Carter: What do you get from petting rabbits with sharp teeth?
Clara: I give up.
Carter: Harecuts.

Carter: What is the difference between here and there?
Clara: You've got me.
Carter: The letter T.

Carter: What would you call a man who is always wiring for money?
Clara: That's a mystery.
Carter: An electrician.

Carter: What is hard to beat?
Clara: I don't have the foggiest.
Carter: A drum with a hole in it.

Carter: What's red and goes up and down?
Clara: I'm in the dark.
Carter: A tomato in an elevator.

Carter: What's red, white, and blue, and has lots of arms?
Clara: Search me.
Carter: An octopus carrying an American flag.

Carter: What is round and purple, travels in a long, black limousine, and carries a machine gun?
Clara: You've got me guessing.
Carter: Al Caplum.

Carter: What do cats read?
Clara: I pass.
Carter: Mews of the World.

Carter: What can speak in every language but never went to school?
Clara: How should I know?
Carter: An echo.

Carter: What age would you be if you were very, very fat?
Clara: I don't know.
Carter: The same age you are now.

Carter: What is an eavesdropper?
Clara: I have no clue.
Carter: An icicle.

Carter: What was the greatest bet ever made?
Clara: I don't know.
Carter: The alpha-bet.

Carter: What works when it plays, and plays when it works?
Clara: I can't guess.
Carter: A fountain.

Carter: What's the best way to catch a squirrel?
Clara: I have no idea.
Carter: Climb a tree and act like a nut.

Carter: What pain do we make light of?
Clara: You tell me.
Carter: Windowpane.

Carter: What was the largest island in the world before Australia was discovered?
Clara: I give up.
Carter: Australia.

Carter: What happens if you get vinegar in your ear?
Clara: Who knows?
Carter: You suffer from pickled hearing.

Carter: What food is dear at any price?
Clara: You've got me.
Carter: Venison.

Carter: What are the three most common causes of forest fires?
Clara: My mind's a blank.
Carter: Men, women, and children.

Carter: What did the nearsighted porcupine say when it backed into a cactus?
Clara: That's a mystery.
Carter: Pardon me, honey.

Carter: What kind of problem does a five-foot man have?
Clara: It's unknown to me.
Carter: He needs two-and-a-half pairs of shoes!

Carter: What do they play in Edinburgh when the sidewalks are too hot?
Clara: I'm in the dark.
Carter: Hopscotch!

Carter: What do turtles give each other?
Clara: Search me.
Carter: People-neck sweaters.

Carter: What is a successful farmer?
Clara: You've got me guessing.
Carter: A man outstanding in his field.

Carter: What was the tow car doing at the auto race?
Clara: I pass.
Carter: Pulling a fast one!

Carter: What did the first shipwrecked sailor say when the second sailor was washed ashore?
Clara: How should I know?
Carter: Now we have two on the isle.

Carter: What did the steak say to the plate?
Clara: I don't know.
Carter: Pleased to meat you.

Carter: What fairy tale character hasn't done his ironing in years?
Clara: I have no clue.
Carter: Rumpelstiltskin.

Carter: Who writes nursery rhymes and squeezes oranges?
Clara: I can't guess.
Carter: Mother Juice.

Carter: I'm on my way to visit my outlaws.
Clara: You mean your in-laws, don't you?
Carter: No—outlaws. They're a bunch of bandits.

Carter: My wife writes me that she is all unstrung. What shall I do?
Clara: You tell me.
Carter: Maybe I should send her a wire.

Carter: I broke my nose in two places.
Clara: You better stay out of those places.

Carter: I lost my dog and I feel awful.
Clara: You must be terrier-stricken.

Carter: I got my dog a flea collar.
Clara: Did he like it?
Carter: No. It ticked him off.

Carter: I have ringing in my ears. What should I do?
Clara: Maybe you should consider getting an unlisted ear.

Carter: I'm going to put you on bread and water as punishment. How would you like that?

Clara: I would like the whole wheat toasted.

Carter: I once shot a lion 15 feet long.

Clara: Some lyin'!

19

Little boy: Daddy, do you think clams are happy?
Father: Have you ever heard one complain?

Moose: I'd like a triple chocolate ice cream sundae with lots of nuts on top of the whipped cream.
Waiter: How about a cherry on top?
Moose: Golly, no! I'm on a diet.

Clayton: Where in the world are you going with that candy bag?
Conrad: I've got a 14-carat diamond ring in it, and I'm goin' to propose to my girl.
Clayton: Do you think she'll accept you?
Conrad: Sure—it's in the bag.

Joe: Are you crazy if you talk to yourself?
Moe: Only if you listen to yourself.

Rex: What is the opposite of sorrow?
Tex: Joy.
Rex: And the opposite of misery?
Tex: Happiness.
Rex: And what is the opposite of woe?
Tex: Giddyap!

Tyler: Did anyone laugh when you fell on the ice?
Travis: No, but the ice made a few cracks.

Zack: I'm exhausted! I was up until midnight doing homework!
Mack: What time did you start?
Zack: Eleven forty-five.

Mother: Sit down and tell me what your grades are in school.
Son: I can't. I just told Pop.

Prison warden: I've been in charge of this prison for ten years. Let's have a celebration. What kind of party do you suggest?
Prisoner: An open house!

Owen: I started life without a penny in my pocket.
Orin: So what? I started life without a pocket!

Mark: Which baseball team do you like best, the Red Sox or the Nylons?
Matt: The Red Sox.
Mark: But the Nylons get more runs!

Randy: I'd go to the ends of the earth for you.
Sandy: Yeah, but would you stay there?

Karl: Did they take an X-ray of your sister Sue's jaw at the hospital?
Kyle: They tried to, but the only thing they could get was a motion picture.

Corey: When I went fishing I saw a fish that weighed 20 pounds jump out of the water.
Carter: How do you know it weighed 20 pounds?
Corey: It had scales on its back.

Jonas: I've changed my mind.
Joshua: Well, it can't be any worse than your old one.

Gabriel: My father can hold up an auto with one hand.
Flora: He must be a very strong man!
Gabriel: Not particularly—he's a policeman!

She: Did you get hurt when you were on the football team?
He: No. It was while the team was on me.

Horace: Did you know that when there's lightning, cows hide in trees?
Harry: I never see them.
Horace: See how good they hide?

Reporter: Why did you go to the North Pole?
Adventurer: Because I wanted to feel on top of the world.

20

Did you hear about the cookie that cried?
His mother had been a wafer too long.

Did you hear about the two hypochondriacs who got together?
They had a hurt-to-hurt conversation.

Did you ever hear the story of the new roof?
It's over your head.

Did you hear the one about the electric eel?
It's shocking!

Did you hear the one about the air conditioner?
It's so cool!

Did you hear the one about the broken pencil?
It's pointless!

Did you hear the one about the helium balloon?
It's a gas!

Did you hear the one about the ruby?
It's a real gem!

Did you hear the one about the electric drill?
It's boring!

Did you hear the one about the redwood?
It's tree-mendous!

Did you hear the one about the owl?
It's a hoot!

Did you hear the one about the snake?
It's hiss-terical!

Did you hear the one about the dynamite?
It's a blast!

Did you hear the one about the frog?
It's toadly hilarious!

Did you hear the one about the tornado?
It'll blow you away!

Did you hear about the woman who cooked thousands of TV dinners?
She thought she was in show business.

Did you hear about the man who got hurt?
No one would go to the store for him, so he ran over himself.

Do you know what Mr. Goodyear is doing now?
He is re-tired.

Did you hear about the kid who was 20 minutes early for school?
He was in a class by himself.

Did you hear about the artist with a poor memory?
He kept drawing a blank.

Did you hear the story about the bed?
It was just made up.

Did you hear about the guy who stole the judge's calendar?
He got 12 months.

Did you hear about the shoplifter at the lingerie shop?
She gave police the slip.

Did you hear about the guy who had his whole left side shot off?
He's all right now.

Did you hear about the successful school play?
It was a class act.

Did you hear about the boardinghouse that blew up?
Roomers were flying.

Say, did you read in the newspaper about the fellow who ate six dozen pancakes at one sitting?
No, how waffle!

Did you know that Nancy married a janitor?
He just swept her off her feet.

Did your watch stop when it fell on the floor?
Sure. Did you think it would go right on through?

21

Ambrose: What nation always wins in the end?
Agatha: I have no clue.
Ambrose: Determination.

Ambrose: What state never has a kind word to say about anyone?
Agatha: I don't know.
Ambrose: Rude Island.

Ambrose: What did the rake say to the hoe?
Agatha: Beats me.
Ambrose: Hi, hoe!

Ambrose: What kind of fish has perfect pitch?
Agatha: I can't guess.
Ambrose: A piano tuna.

Ambrose: What is a sleeping child?
Agatha: I have no idea.
Ambrose: A kidnapper.

Ambrose: What do you get if you cross a kangaroo and an elephant?
Agatha: You tell me.
Ambrose: Giant holes all over Australia!

Ambrose: What is brown, hairy, and wears sunglasses?
Agatha: I give up.
Ambrose: A coconut on vacation.

Ambrose: What can you make that no one can see?
Agatha: Who knows?
Ambrose: A noise.

Ambrose: What's the easiest way to widen a road?
Agatha: You've got me.
Ambrose: Just add a B and it becomes broad right away.

Ambrose: What did the rose say to the bee?
Agatha: My mind's a blank.
Ambrose: Buzz off!

Ambrose: What do you call a man who likes throwing things?
Agatha: That's a mystery.
Ambrose: Chuck.

Ambrose: What part of the body do ticks like to bite?
Agatha: I'm blank.
Ambrose: Ticks attack toes.

Ambrose: What would the duckling say if it saw an orange in its nest?
Agatha: I don't have the foggiest.
Ambrose: Look at the orange marmalade (mama laid)!

Ambrose: What happened to the plastic surgeon when he warmed his hands in front of the fire?
Agatha: It's unknown to me.
Ambrose: He melted.

Ambrose: What do you get if you cross a centipede and a parrot?
Agatha: I'm in the dark.
Ambrose: A walkie-talkie.

Ambrose: What never asks questions but gets pressed for answers?
Agatha: Search me.
Ambrose: A doorbell.

Ambrose: What do you call a rabbit that likes to swim with alligators?
Agatha: I pass.
Ambrose: Dinner.

Ambrose: What is that selfish girl's name?
Agatha: I don't know.
Ambrose: Mimi.

Ambrose: What does a cat like to eat at breakfast time?
Agatha: I have no clue.
Ambrose: Mice crispies.

Ambrose: What kind of bugs live at the very bottom of the ocean?
Agatha: I don't know.
Ambrose: Wet ones.

Ambrose: What kind of dress did Cinderella wear to the ball?
Agatha: I have no clue.
Ambrose: She wore a wish-and-wear dress.

Ambrose: What is blind itself, yet guides the blind?
Agatha: I don't know.
Ambrose: A walking stick.

Ambrose: What table is made of paper?
Agatha: Beats me.
Ambrose: A timetable.

Ambrose: What is the best way to hide a bear?
Agatha: I can't guess.
Ambrose: Skin him.

Ambrose: What is in the Great Wall of China that the Chinese never put there?
Agatha: I have no idea.
Ambrose: Cracks.

Ambrose: What makes the Tower of Pisa lean?
Agatha: You tell me.
Ambrose: It doesn't eat enough.

Ambrose: What is the difference between a greedy person and an electric toaster?
Agatha: I give up.
Ambrose: One takes the most, and the other makes the toast.

Ambrose: What did the jack say to the car?
Agatha: Who knows?
Ambrose: Can I give you a lift?

Ambrose: What fruit kept best in Noah's ark?
Agatha: That's a mystery.
Ambrose: The preserved pears (pairs).

Ambrose: What goes into the water white and comes out blue?
Agatha: I'm blank.
Ambrose: A swimmer on a cold day.

Ambrose: What do bees do with their honey?
Agatha: I don't have the foggiest.
Ambrose: They cell it.

Ambrose: What did one windshield wiper say to the other one?
Agatha: It's unknown to me.
Ambrose: Isn't it a shame we meet only when it rains?

Ambrose: What is a piece of Italian pie?
Agatha: I'm in the dark.
Ambrose: A pizza pie.

Ambrose: What is a twip?
Agatha: Search me.
Ambrose: A twip is what a wabbit takes when he wides a too-too twain.

Ambrose: What did the boy say when the dentist asked him what kind of filling he wanted?
Agatha: I pass.
Ambrose: Chocolate!

Ambrose: What is a clumsy Santa Claus?
Agatha: How should I know?
Ambrose: A Santa Klutz.

Ambrose: What are the six main seasons?
Agatha: I have no clue.
Ambrose: Summer, fall, winter, spring, salt, and pepper.

Ambrose: What is a ringleader?
Agatha: I don't know.
Ambrose: The first person in the bathtub.

Ambrose: What did the farmer say when he saw three ducks in his mailbox?
Agatha: I have no clue.
Ambrose: Bills, bills, bills.

Ambrose: What happened to the two silkworms who had a race?
Agatha: Beats me.
Ambrose: They ended up in a tie.

Ambrose: What is a navel destroyer?
Agatha: I can't guess.
Ambrose: A hula hoop with a nail in it.

Ambrose: What is white and lifts weights?
Agatha: I have no idea.
Ambrose: An extra-strength aspirin.

Ambrose: What did Humpty Dumpty do after the fall?
Agatha: You tell me.
Ambrose: He called his lawyer.

Ambrose: What does a pig put on himself when he gets a sunburn?
Agatha: I give up.
Ambrose: Oinkment.

Ambrose: What job does a loon do in the forest?
Agatha: Who knows?
Ambrose: He's a loon ranger.

Ambrose: What does it take to be a plumber?
Agatha: You've got me.
Ambrose: Pipe dreams.

Ambrose: What fruit is always complaining?
Agatha: That's a mystery.
Ambrose: A crabapple.

Ambrose: How do you make a breadstick?
Agatha: I have no clue.
Ambrose: Use a lot of glue.

Ambrose: How can you recognize a gypsy moth?
Agatha: Beats me.
Ambrose: It tries to tell your fortune.

Ambrose: How many wheels does a car have?
Agatha: I can't guess.
Ambrose: Six, including the steering wheel and spare tire.

Ambrose: How do hot dogs speak?
Agatha: I have no idea.
Ambrose: Frankly.

Ambrose: How did the prisoner escape?
Agatha: You tell me.
Ambrose: He broke out with the measles.

Ambrose: How did the dove save so much money?
Agatha: I give up.
Ambrose: By using coopons.

Ambrose: How do you catch a unique bunny?
Agatha: Who knows?
Ambrose: Unique up on him.

Ambrose: How do you catch a tame bunny?
Agatha: You've got me.
Ambrose: The tame way.

Ambrose: How would you punctuate the sentence: "I saw a five dollar bill on the sidewalk"?
Agatha: My mind is blank.
Ambrose: I'd make a dash after it.

Ambrose: How do you catch celery?
Agatha: That's a mystery.
Ambrose: You stalk it.

Ambrose: How did you get rid of the bloodhounds trailing us?
Agatha: I threw a penny in the stream, and they followed the cent.

Eileen: How do you get rid of bedbugs?
Olivia: I have no clue.
Eileen: Make them sleep on the couch.

Eileen: How do you make a kitchen sink?
Olivia: Beats me.
Eileen: Throw it into the ocean.

Eileen: How can you tell if a lobster is fresh?
Olivia: I can't guess.
Eileen: If he tries to kiss you.

Eileen: How do you make a strawberry shake?
Olivia: I have no idea.
Eileen: Sneak up on it and say, "Boo!"

Eileen: How is the archaeologist doing?
Olivia: You tell me.
Eileen: Her life's work is in ruins.

Eileen: How much does it cost for an elephant to get a haircut?
Olivia: I give up.
Eileen: Five dollars for the haircut and five hundred dollars for the chair.

Eileen: How did you find the lost leopard?
Olivia: I just spotted him.

Eileen: How much sand would be in a hole one foot long, one foot wide, and one foot deep?
Olivia: You've got me.
Eileen: None, silly. There is no sand in a hole.

Eileen: How do you keep a rhinoceros from charging?
Olivia: My mind is blank.
Eileen: Take away his credit card.

Eileen: Which is the bossiest type of ant?
Olivia: I have no clue.
Eileen: Tyrant.

Eileen: Which ant is an army officer?
Olivia: Beats me.
Eileen: Sergeant.

Eileen: Where was Captain Kidd's chest buried?
Olivia: I have no idea.
Eileen: With the rest of his body.

Eileen: Where do they keep the kettle on a ship?
Olivia: You tell me.
Eileen: In the boiler room.

Eileen: Where do you buy a comb?
Olivia: I give up.
Eileen: At a parts store.

Eileen: Where does Saint Nick go on holidays?
Olivia: Who knows?
Eileen: On a Santa Cruise.

Eileen: Where do they keep all the pigs in Oregon?
Olivia: You've got me.
Eileen: In the state pen.

Eileen: Where does a cow go on Saturday night?
Olivia: My mind is blank.
Eileen: To the moo-vies.

Eileen: Where do you learn how to scoop ice cream?
Olivia: That's a mystery.
Eileen: At sundae school.

Eileen: Where is the place where part of the family waits until the others are through with the car?
Olivia: I don't know.
Eileen: Home.

Eileen: When are roads unpleasant?
Olivia: Search me.
Eileen: When they are crossroads.

Eileen: When is a car like a frog?
Olivia: I don't have the foggiest.
Eileen: When it's being toad.

Eileen: When Big Chief Shortcake died, what did his widow do?
Olivia: I'm in the dark.
Eileen: Squaw bury Shortcake.

23

Knock, knock.
Who's there?
Ether.
Ether who?
Ether bunny.

Knock, knock.
Who's there?
Tick.
Tick who?
Tick um up. I'm a tongue-tied cowboy.

Knock, knock.
Who's there?
Jess.
Jess who?
Jess little old me.

Knock, knock.
Who's there?
Red.
Red who?
Red pepper. Isn't that a hot one?

Knock, knock.
Who's there?
Ooze.
Ooze who?
Ooze in charge around here?

Knock, knock.
Who's there?
Frankfurter.
Frankfurter who?
Frankfurter memories.

Knock, knock.
Who's there?
Shelby.
Shelby who?
Shelby comin' 'round the mountain when she comes.

Knock, knock.
Who's there?
Wendy.
Wendy who?
Wendy joke is over, you had better laugh.

Knock, knock.
Who's there?
Distress.
Distress who?
Distress is very short.

Knock, knock.
Who's there?
Toodle.
Toodle who?
Toodle who to you, too!

Knock, knock.
Who's there?
Barbie.
Barbie who?
Barbie Q Chicken.

Knock, knock.
Who's there?
Roach.
Roach who?
Roach you a letter, did you get it?

Knock, knock.
Who's there?
Carmen.
Carmen who?
Carmen to my parlor, said the spider to the fly.

Knock, knock.
Who's there?
Altoona.
Altoona who?
Altoona piano and you play it.

Knock, knock.
Who's there?
House.
House who?
House it going?

Knock, knock.
Who's there?
Lettuce.
Lettuce who?
Lettuce discuss this like mature adults.

Knock, knock.
Who's there?
Albee.
Albee who?
Albee a monkey's uncle!

Knock, knock.
Who's there?
Wanda.
Wanda who?
Wanda come out and play?

Knock, knock.
Who's there?
Sherwood.
Sherwood who?
Sherwood like to come in.

Knock, knock.
Who's there?
Isabel.
Isabel who?
Isabel busted?

Knock, knock.
Who's there?
Tank.
Tank who?
Tank you for coming to the door.

Knock, knock.
Who's there?
Kleenex.
Kleenex who?
Kleenex are prettier than dirty necks.

Knock, knock.
Who's there?
Despair.
Despair who?
Despair of shoes is too tight.

Knock, knock.
Who's there?
Harry.
Harry who?
Harry up, it's cold out here.

Knock, knock.
Who's there?
Hugh.
Hugh who?
Well, yoo-hoo to you too!

Knock, knock.
Who's there?
Major.
Major who?
Major open the door!

Knock, knock.
Who's there?
Mark.
Mark who?
Mark the herald angels sing!

Knock, knock.
Who's there?
Ben.
Ben who?
Ben walkin' the dog.

Knock, knock.
Who's there?
Howard.
Howard who?
Howard you like to be my Valentine?

Knock, knock.
Who's there?
Norma Lee.
Norma Lee who?
Norma Lee I don't ring other people's doorbells.

Knock, knock.
Who's there?
Phyllis.
Phyllis who?
Phyllis in on the news.

Knock, knock.
Who's there?
Hume.
Hume who?
Hume do you expect?

Knock, knock.
Who's there?
Iran.
Iran who?
Iran up the stairs and I'm outta breath.

Knock, knock.
Who's there?
Norma Lee.
Norma Lee who?
Norma Lee we go swimming on Sundays, but
I thought we'd see you instead.

Knock, knock.
Who's there?
Diploma.
Diploma who?
Diploma to fix da leak.

Knock, knock.
Who's there?
Sultan.
Sultan who?
Sultan pepper.

Knock, knock.
Who's there?
Yah.
Yah who?
Gosh, I'm glad to see you too!

Knock, knock.
Who's there?
Nana.
Nana who?
Nana your business.

24

Academy Awards: A place where everyone lets off esteem.

Adolescent: A youngster who is old enough to dress himself if he could just remember where he dropped his clothes.

Alarm clock: A frightened timepiece.

Antique shop: A junk store that has raised its prices.

Applause: Two hands slapping each other's faces.

Atoll: What you pay before you cross a bridge.

Author: A person who is usually write.

Awe: Wow of silence.

Bad driver: The person you run into.

Badmutton: Game played with the butcher.

Bedrock: Any rocks you find in your bed.

Blackmail: A letter dropped in a mud puddle.

Cabbage: The age of a taxi.

Cartoon: A song sung in an automobile.

Circle: A round line with a hole in the middle.

Coincide: What you should do when it rains.

College cheer: Money from home.

Comedian: A person with a pun-track mind.

Compliment: The applause that refreshes.

Conscience: What makes you worry about what it couldn't stop you from doing.

Editor: A literary barber.

Embezzlement: Bankers away!

Eureka: A euphemism for "you smell bad."

Exclamation point: A period that has blown its top.

Eyedropper: A very, very careless person.

Eyes: Double feature.

Filing cabinet: A place where you lose things alphabetically.

Finland: A place where many sharks live.

Fireproof: The boss's relatives.

Flabbergasted: The state you are in when you're overwhelmed by a flabber.

Flashlight: A case in which to carry dead batteries.

Flood: A river that's too big for its bridges.

Forger: A person who is always ready to write a wrong.

Frustration: What happens when a mosquito bites a turnip.

Gossip: One who takes in rumors.

Halo: A greeting used by angels.

Handicap: A ready-to-wear hat.

High heels: An invention by a girl who was kissed on the forehead one too many times.

Hypodermic needle: A sick-shooter.

Jealousy: The friendship one woman has for another.

Jump: The last word in airplanes.

Kiss: Something that is taken at face value.

Laugh: A smile that burst.

Laundress: A gown worn while sitting on the grass.

Lawsuit: Generally a loss-suit.

Love: A heart attack.

Martyr: A self-made hero.

Meditation: Inner calm system.

Minority rule: A baby in the house.

Mischief: The chief's daughter.

Moon: A sky light.

Mud pack: Self-putty.

Nitrate: Cheapest price for calling long distance.

Nursery: Bawl room.

Old timer: A person who remembers when you didn't start to shop for Christmas until after Thanksgiving.

Paralyze: Two untruths.

Parasols: Two men named Sol.

Pipe-cleaner: A toothpick with long underwear.

Prisoner: A bird in a guilty cage.

Punctuality: The best way to avoid meeting people.

Quadruplets: Four crying out loud.

Raving beauty: The second place winner in a beauty contest.

Scotland Yard: Three feet, the same as everywhere else.

Screen door: Something the kids get a bang out of.

Shopper: Someone who likes to go buy-buy.

Snoring: Sheet music.

Spanking: Stern punishment.

Surfing: A tide ride.

Sweater: A garment worn by a small child when his mother feels chilly.

Television: Chewing gum for the eyes.

Thief: A person who finds things before the owner loses them.

Timekeeper: A clock-eyed man.

Twins: Infant replay.

Waiter: A man who believes money grows on trays.

Work: An unpopular way to earn money.

25

Barnaby: What's wrong with overeating?
Barbie: Search me.
Barnaby: It makes you thick to your stomach.

Barnaby: When does a farmer have the best chance to see his pigs?
Barbie: You've got me guessing.
Barnaby: When he has a sty in his eye.

Barnaby: What is found in the center of America and Australia?
Barbie: Beats me.
Barnaby: The letter R.

Barnaby: Why didn't Eve have any sisters?
Barbie: I have no clue.
Barnaby: Because Adam had no spare ribs.

Barnaby: Why is it a good idea to have holes in your jeans?
Barbie: I don't know.
Barnaby: So you can get your legs inside.

Barnaby: What is a cat's skin used for?
Barbie: I have no idea.
Barnaby: To hold the cat together.

Barnaby: What is incredibly intelligent, weighs 200 pounds, and is made out of iron?
Barbie: You tell me.
Barnaby: Albert Einstein Dumbbell.

Barnaby: What climbs trees, stores nuts for the winter, and weighs three tons?
Barbie: I give up.
Barnaby: A crazy elephant who thinks he is a squirrel.

Barnaby: What locomotive wears sneakers?
Barbie: Who knows?
Barnaby: A shoe-shoe train.

Barnaby: What do you call great bodies of water filled with grape juice?
Barbie: That's a mystery.
Barnaby: The Grape Lakes.

Barnaby: What do patriotic monkeys wave on Flag Day?
Barbie: Tell me.
Barnaby: Star-Spangled bananas.

Barnaby: What is harder than catching a train when you're late?
Barbie: I don't have the foggiest.
Barnaby: Throwing one.

Barnaby: What happens to Whistler's mother when she works too hard?
Barbie: It's unknown to me.
Barnaby: She goes off her rocker.

Barnaby: What kind of car does Elsie the Cow drive?
Barbie: My mind is a blank.
Barnaby: A moo-ving van.

Barnaby: What state is necessary for dirty clothes?
Barbie: I'm in the dark.
Barnaby: Wash.

Barnaby: What is it called when you holler to a person two miles away?
Barbie: Search me.
Barnaby: Lung distance.

Barnaby: Who was the famous chicken who rode with the Rough Riders and later became president?
Barbie: Beats me.
Barnaby: Teddy Roostervelt.

Barnaby: Where do frogs hang up their coats?
Barbie: I can't guess.
Barnaby: In the croakroom.

Barnaby: Why did Elsie the Cow go to Hollywood?
Barbie: I have no clue.
Barnaby: To be a moo-vie star.

Barnaby: Why don't rabbits need calculators?
Barbie: I don't know.
Barnaby: Because they can multiply quickly without them.

Barnaby: What game do rabbits always love to play?
Barbie: You tell me.
Barnaby: Hopscotch.

Barnaby: What's black and white and pink all over?
Barbie: I give up.
Barnaby: An embarrassed zebra.

Barnaby: What cowboy steals teapots?
Barbie: That's a mystery.
Barnaby: A kettle rustler.

Barnaby: What business is King Kong in?
Barbie: Who knows?
Barnaby: Monkey business.

Barnaby: What word of three syllables is always mispronounced?
Barbie: I have no idea.
Barnaby: Mispronounced.

Barnaby: What do short fairy tale characters wear to look taller?
Barbie: You've got me.
Barnaby: Rumpel-stilts.

Barnaby: What dancer spins straw into gold?
Barbie: My mind is a blank.
Barnaby: Rhumba-stiltskin.

Barnaby: What did Ali Baba write on?
Barbie: Tell me.
Barnaby: Sandpaper.

Barnaby: What state would a gold prospector like?
Barbie: It's unknown to me.
Barnaby: Ore.

Barnaby: What state do you use when you talk about yourself?
Barbie: I don't have the foggiest.
Barnaby: Me.

Barnaby: What state is a church service?
Barbie: I'm in the dark.
Barnaby: Mass.

Barnaby: What did Sir Lancelot wear to bed?
Barbie: Search me.
Barnaby: A knight gown.

Barnaby: Why did the otter cross the road?
Barbie: Beats me.
Barnaby: He didn't want to be mistaken for a chicken.

Barnaby: Why couldn't the crab learn to share?
Barbie: I can't guess.
Barnaby: Because it was shellfish.

Barnaby: What is the difference between a lizard, a crybaby, and a roadrunner?
Barbie: I don't know.
Barnaby: One creeps, one weeps, and one beeps.

Barnaby: What did the thief name his son?
Barbie: I have no idea.
Barnaby: Robin.

Barnaby: What is impossible to hold for half an hour even though it's lighter than air?
Barbie: You tell me.
Barnaby: Your breath.

Barnaby: What is the world's craziest satellite?
Barbie: It's unknown to me.
Barnaby: A fool moon.

Barnaby: What ape helped settle the American frontier?
Barbie: I give up.
Barnaby: Daniel Ba-Boone.

Barnaby: What do you call short stories written by hogs?
Barbie: Who knows?
Barnaby: Pig tales.

Barnaby: What do 500-pound canaries do on Sundays?
Barbie: My mind is a blank.
Barnaby: They go to chirp.

Barnaby: What is the best-looking geometric figure?
Barbie: That's a mystery.
Barnaby: Acute angle.

Barnaby: What do you get when you use soap and water on the stove?
Barbie: Tell me.
Barnaby: Foam on the range.

Barnaby: What is the craziest and cheapest way to buy holes?
Barbie: I don't have the foggiest.
Barnaby: Wholesale.

Barnaby: Why was the shad turned down by the army?
Barbie: How should I know?
Barnaby: He failed his herring test.

Barnaby: What do you get when you cross a lighthouse and a henhouse?
Barbie: Beats me.
Barnaby: Beacon and eggs.

Barnaby: What does a nearsighted gingerbread man use for eyes?
Barbie: I can't guess.
Barnaby: Contact raisins.

Barnaby: What shampoo do mountains use?
Barbie: Give me the answer.
Barnaby: Head and Boulders.

Barnaby: What part of the car is first to get weary?
Barbie: I don't know.
Barnaby: The tires.

Barnaby: What is yellow, swims in the ocean, and swallows ships?
Barbie: I have no idea.
Barnaby: Moby Banana.

Barnaby: What did the adding machine say to the clerk?
Barbie: You tell me.
Barnaby: You can count on me.

Barnaby: What did the apple tree say to the farmer?
Barbie: I give up.
Barnaby: Why don't you stop picking on me?

Barnaby: What do crows sail in?
Barbie: That's a mystery.
Barnaby: Crowboats.

Barnaby: Why do people stand on two legs?
Barbie: I have no clue.
Barnaby: If they didn't, they would fall over.

Barnaby: Why did the two fish get married?
Barbie: Beats me.
Barnaby: Because they were hooked on each other.

Barnaby: Why was the lifeguard at the store?
Barbie: I can't guess.
Barnaby: He heard he could save a lot.

Barnaby: Why is it never good to swim on an empty stomach?
Barbie: I have no idea.
Barnaby: Because it's easier to swim in water.

Barnaby: Why are you so mad?
Barbie: I brought my leopard-skin coat to the cleaners.
Barnaby: What's wrong with that?
Barbie: It came back spotless.

Barnaby: Why didn't the elephant buy a small sports car?
Barbie: I give up.
Barnaby: It had no trunk space.

Barnaby: How did the carpenter break all his teeth?
Barbie: Who knows?
Barnaby: From chewing his nails.

Barnaby: Why did the seal cross the road?
Barbie: You've got me.
Barnaby: To get to the otter side.

Barnaby: Why didn't the kitchen window like the living room window?
Barbie: My mind is blank.
Barnaby: Because it was such a big pane.

Barnaby: Why was the weatherman arrested?
Barbie: That's a mystery.
Barnaby: For shooting the breeze.

Barnaby: Why did the rooster refuse to fight?
Barbie: I don't know.
Barnaby: He was chicken.

26

Lola: What animals are poor dancers?
Lionel: I have no clue.
Lola: Four-legged ones, because they have two left feet.

Lola: What makes everyone sick except those who swallow it?
Lionel: Beats me.
Lola: Flattery.

Lola: What book contains more stirring pages than any other?
Lionel: I can't guess.
Lola: A cookbook.

Lola: What criminal doesn't take a bath?
Lionel: I have no idea.
Lola: A dirty crook.

Lola: What kind of person loves cocoa?
Lionel: You tell me.
Lola: A coconut.

Lola: What do you get if you cross a raccoon with a kangaroo?
Lionel: I give up.
Lola: A fur coat with pockets.

Lola: What did the cotton plant say to the farmer?
Lionel: Who knows?
Lola: Stop picking on me.

Lola: What is a gossip's favorite cake?
Lionel: You've got me.
Lola: Spice cake.

Lola: What should I wear with yellow, green, and purple socks?
Lionel: My mind's a blank.
Lola: Hip boots!

Lola: What can you play on a shoehorn?
Lionel: That's a mystery.
Lola: Sole music!

Lola: What is a midget skunk called?
Lionel: I'm blank.
Lola: A shrunk skunk.

Lola: What kind of cow goes "Beeeeeeeep beeeeeeeep"?
Lionel: I don't have the foggiest.
Lola: A longhorn!

Lola: What happened to the man who stole ten bars of soap?
Lionel: I'm in the dark.
Lola: He made a clean getaway.

Lola: What do you get when you cross a dog with an elephant?
Lionel: Search me.
Lola: A very nervous mail carrier.

Lola: What travels underground at 80 miles an hour?
Lionel: I pass.
Lola: A mole on a motorbike.

Lola: What has two heads, four eyes, six legs, and a tail?
Lionel: How should I know?
Lola: A horse and rider.

Lola: What can you put into a glass bottle but never take out?
Lionel: I don't know.
Lola: A crack.

Lola: What lies at the bottom of the sea and wriggles?
Lionel: I have no clue.
Lola: A nervous wreck.

Lola: What did the balloon say to the pin?
Lionel: I have no clue.
Lola: Hello, buster.

Lola: What's a good pet for a conceited actor?
Lionel: I don't know.
Lola: A hamster!

Lola: What's big, purple, and lies across the sea from us?
Lionel: Beats me.
Lola: Grape Britain.

Lola: What do you call a male owl?
Lionel: I can't guess.
Lola: A wise guy.

Lola: What is big, likes peanuts, and has a trunk?
Lionel: I have no idea.
Lola: An oak tree with a squirrel in it.

Lola: What do you get when you cross a poodle and a cuckoo clock?
Lionel: You tell me.
Lola: A watchdog.

Lola: What were the highest mountains in Europe before the Alps were discovered?
Lionel: I give up.
Lola: The Alps, of course.

Lola: What's another name for counterfeit money?
Lionel: Who knows?
Lola: Homemade bread.

Lola: What vegetable was known as "The King of Rock 'n' Roll"?
Lionel: You've got me.
Lola: Elvis Parsley!

Lola: What is the definition of impossible?
Lionel: That's a mystery.
Lola: Trying to pull a hair off a flea with boxing gloves on.

Lola: What do you get if you cross a ham and a karate expert?
Lionel: I don't have the foggiest.
Lola: Pork chops.

Lola: What is the difference between a girl and a horse?
Lionel: It's unknown to me.
Lola: I'll bet you have some swell dates.

Lola: What did the golf ball say to the golf club?
Lionel: I'm blank.
Lola: You drive me wild!

Lola: What's another name for a cowhand?
Lionel: I'm in the dark.
Lola: Hamburger helper!

Lola: What carries things but does not move?
Lionel: Search me.
Lola: A shelf.

Lola: What kind of dog would a chemistry professor have?
Lionel: You've got me guessing.
Lola: A laboratory retriever.

Lola: What is the best name for the wife of a marksman?
Lionel: I pass.
Lola: Amy.

Lola: What is the happiest state in the union?
Lionel: How should I know?
Lola: Merryland.

Lola: Which is the dumbest ant?
Lionel: I have no clue.
Lola: Ignorant.

Lola: Which is the biggest ant?
Lionel: Beats me.
Lola: Elephant.

Lola: Which rabbit stole from the rich to give to the poor?
Lionel: I can't guess.
Lola: Rabbit Hood.

Lola: Where does a skunk sit in church?
Lionel: I have no idea.
Lola: In a pew (phew).

Lola: Where do you go to become a smart prisoner?
Lionel: Who knows?
Lola: Go directly to Yale.

Lola: Where does a track star keep his money?
Lionel: You've got me.
Lola: In a pole vault.

Lola: Where is Captain Hook's treasure chest?
Lionel: My mind is blank.
Lola: Under his treasure shirt.

Lola: Where does the king keep his army?
Lionel: That's a mystery.
Lola: Up his sleevey.

Lola: Where do rabbits go when they get married?
Lionel: I don't know.
Lola: On their bunnymoon.

Lola: Where was the first french fry made?
Lionel: Search me.
Lola: In Greece.

Lola: When is the best time for a farmer to retire?
Lionel: I don't have the foggiest.
Lola: About nine o'clock.

Lola: When is an operation funny?
Lionel: I'm in the dark.
Lola: When it leaves the patient in stitches.

Lola: When rain falls, does it ever get up again?
Lionel: You've got me guessing.
Lola: Oh, yes—in dew time.

Lola: What do you call 300 rabbits marching backward?
Lionel: I have no clue.
Lola: A receding hareline.

Lola: What do you call a tire salesperson?
Lionel: Beats me.
Lola: A wheeler-dealer.

Lola: What is a musician's favorite dessert?
Lionel: I can't guess.
Lola: Cello.

Lola: What is the auto parts store slogan?
Lionel: I have no idea.
Lola: You deserve a brake today.

Lola: What did the police say when a famous drawing was stolen?
Lionel: You tell me.
Lola: Details are sketchy.

Lola: What has a long neck, a well-known name, and wears a cap?
Lionel: I give up.
Lola: A bottle.

Lola: What did the barber call his son?
Lionel: Who knows?
Lola: A little shaver.

Lola: What goes tock-tick?
Lionel: You've got me.
Lola: A backward clock.

Lola: What did the coffee say to the police?
Lionel: My mind is blank.
Lola: I've been mugged.

Lola: What do you say to curtains?
Lionel: That's a mystery.
Lola: Pull yourself together.

In what way was Ruth very rude to Boaz?
She pulled his ears and trod on his corn.

In what place did the cock crow so that all the world could hear him?
On Noah's ark.

Where do you think the Israelites may have deposited their money?
At the banks of the Jordan.

What was the most expensive meal served in the Bible, and who ate it?
Esau. It cost him his birthright—Genesis 25:34.

Why did Noah have to punish and discipline the chickens on the ark?
Because they were using fowl language.

Why was Job always cold in bed?
Because he had such miserable comforters.

What wages can't you spend?
The wages of sin.

What were the Phoenicians famous for?
Blinds.

Where did Noah strike the first nail in the ark?
On the head.

At what time of day was Adam born?
A little before eve.

What man in the Bible had no parents?
Joshua, the son of Nun.

Why are there so few men with whiskers in heaven?
Because most men get in by a close shave.

A man was just admitted to the hospital for surgery. He said to his doctor, "I'm so frightened. This is my first operation."

The doctor nodded his head and replied, "I know just how you feel. It's my first operation too!"

A small boy stood in the entrance to the cobbler's shop watching the man at work.

Boy: What do you repair boots with, mister?

Cobbler: Hide.

Boy: What?

Cobbler: I said hide!

Boy: Huh?

Cobbler: I said hide!

Boy: What for?

Cobbler: Hide! The cow's outside.

Boy: Don't care if it is. Who's afraid of a cow, anyway?

Jamie: It must be kind of difficult to eat soup with a beard!
Warren: Yes, it's quite a strain!

Roses are red,
And your face is so pink;
Which proves you should speak
Only after you think.

A kangaroo was complaining to his psychiatrist: "I don't know what's the matter with me. I just don't feel jumpy anymore."

The movie I just saw shouldn't have been rated PG. It should have been rated RR—for rotten and ridiculous!

The next time you are discouraged and feeling sort of blue, take a look at the mighty oak, and see what a nut can do.

A young boy's parents had paid a visit to the home of a neighbor one evening. When she answered the doorbell the next morning and found the boy at the door, the neighbor thought his parents had forgotten something.

"Please, Mrs. Anderson," said the boy, "may I look at your dining room rug?"

The woman was surprised but said, "Why, of course, Keith. Come right in."

The lad gazed at the rug for several minutes. Then he turned to its owner: "It doesn't make me sick," he said.

With which hand should you stir your çocoa?
With either, but it is better to stir it with a spoon.

If a young boy should lose his knee, where would he go to get another?
To a butcher shop, where kid-neys are sold.

Teacher: Please name the four seasons.
Student: Duck season, rabbit season, deer season, and pheasant season.

A duck was swimming in a pond, and a cat was sitting on its tail. How could that be?
The cat was on the shore sitting on its own tail.

The teacher asked the class to draw a ring. But Ryan drew a square instead. "Why did you draw a square when I asked for a ring?" she said.
"It's a boxing ring."

Teacher: Please name the four seasons.
Student: Salt, pepper, garlic, and mustard.

There was only one piece of cake left on the plate, and Mama divided it between Barnaby and Lola. Barnaby looked at his mother's empty plate and said, "Mama, I can't enjoy my cake when you're not having any. Take Lola's."

Ichabod: When can you spell crazy using just one letter?
Eutychus: Beats me.
Ichabod: When it's U!

Ichabod: Which traffic light is the bravest?
Eutychus: I can't guess.
Ichabod: The one that doesn't turn yellow.

Ichabod: Why did the frog get kicked out of the navy?
Eutychus: I don't know.
Ichabod: He kept jumping ship.

Ichabod: What are the odds of something crazy happening at 12:50?
Eutychus: I have no idea.
Ichabod: Ten-to-one.

Ichabod: What is the biggest soda in the world?
Eutychus: You tell me.
Ichabod: Minnesota.

Ichabod: What happens to dogs who chase cars?
Eutychus: Who knows?
Ichabod: They end up exhausted.

Ichabod: What cultivates the earth and gives milk?
Eutychus: You've got me.
Ichabod: Bossie the Plow.

Ichabod: Why did the frog sit on the lily pad?
Eutychus: I have no clue.
Ichabod: Her sofa was being repaired.

Ichabod: What does an Eskimo put on his bed?
Eutychus: My mind is a blank.
Ichabod: A sheet of ice and a blanket of snow.

Ichabod: What has brown fur, wears a ranger's hat, and hangs from a tree?
Eutychus: That's a mystery.
Ichabod: Smokey Pear.

Ichabod: What's another name for a dining car?
Eutychus: Tell me.
Ichabod: A chew-chew train.

Ichabod: What is orange and half a mile high?
Eutychus: I don't have the foggiest.
Ichabod: The Empire State Carrot.

Ichabod: What did you do last summer?
Eutychus: I worked for an elevator company.
Ichabod: I'll bet that had its ups and downs.

Ichabod: What state is a doctor?
Eutychus: I'm in the dark.
Ichabod: MD.

Ichabod: What fruit studies for exams in a hurry?
Eutychus: Search me.
Ichabod: Cramberries.

Ichabod: If five dogs are chasing a cat down the street, what time is it?
Eutychus: I have no clue.
Ichabod: Five after one.

Ichabod: A zebra with wide stripes married a zebra with narrow stripes. Their first son had no stripes. What did they call him?
Eutychus: Beats me.
Ichabod: Howard.

Ichabod: What is the main ingredient of dog biscuits?
Eutychus: You tell me.
Ichabod: Collie-flour.

Ichabod: If a skunk got its nose cut off, how would it smell?
Eutychus: I don't know.
Ichabod: As bad as ever.

Ichabod: Is the joker animal, vegetable, or mineral?
Eutychus: I can't guess.
Ichabod: Vegetable...he's a human bean.

Ichabod: Where do giant condors come from?
Eutychus: I have no idea.
Ichabod: Eggs.

Ichabod: Where did the joker wind up for stealing shellfish?
Eutychus: I give up.
Ichabod: Small clams court.

Ichabod: Where does the joker fill his car's gas tank?
Eutychus: Who knows?
Ichabod: At the villain station.

Ichabod: When is it proper to go to bed with your shoes on?
Eutychus: You've got me.
Ichabod: When you are a horse.

Ichabod: When is a horse not a horse?
Eutychus: That's a mystery.
Ichabod: When he turns into a barn.

Ichabod: Who is safe when a man-eating tiger is loose?
Eutychus: I'm blank.
Ichabod: Women and children.

Ichabod: Did you ever see a catfish?
Eutychus: No, but I saw a horsefly.

Ichabod: Did you hear about the cat who swallowed the duck?
Eutychus: Nope.
Ichabod: She became a duck-filled fatty-puss.

Ichabod: Did you hear about the cat who swallowed the ball of yarn?
Eutychus: I'm in the dark.
Ichabod: She had mittens.

Ichabod: Did you like the story about the dog who ran two miles just to pick up a stick?
Eutychus: No, I thought it was a little farfetched!

Ichabod: What is gray, has four legs, a tail, and a trunk?
Eutychus: I have no clue.
Ichabod: A mouse going on a trip.

Ichabod: What bird can lift the heaviest weight?
Eutychus: I don't know.
Ichabod: The crane.

Ichabod: What has blonde hair, a gorgeous dress, and a 30-pound stuffed turkey?
Eutychus: Beats me.
Ichabod: Beauty and the Feast.

Ichabod: What is the least dangerous kind of robbery?
Eutychus: I can't guess.
Ichabod: Safe robbery.

Ichabod: What's the difference between a cloud on a rainy day and a boy who is being spanked?
Eutychus: You tell me.
Ichabod: One pours out rain and the other roars out with pain.

Ichabod: What do you call it when you eat three desserts?
Eutychus: I give up.
Ichabod: Cutting back.

Ichabod: What's the difference between an orange and a yo-yo?
Eutychus: Who knows?
Ichabod: You'd be a fine one to send out for oranges.

Ichabod: What has four legs, a curly tail, and an IQ of 200?
Eutychus: You've got me.
Ichabod: Albert Einswine!

Ichabod: What barbarian conqueror was also a male model?
Eutychus: My mind is blank.
Ichabod: Attila the Hunk!

Ichabod: What do you call it when a rock group goes on welfare?
Eutychus: That's a mystery.
Ichabod: Band-Aid.

Ichabod: What time is it when a pie is equally divided among four hungry boys?
Eutychus: I don't have the foggiest.
Ichabod: A quarter to one.

Ichabod: What is the best name for the wife of a real-estate man?
Eutychus: It's unknown to me.
Ichabod: Lottie.

Ichabod: What part of London is in France?
Eutychus: I'm blank.
Ichabod: The letter N.

Ichabod: What are men's opinions of riding skirts?
Eutychus: I'm in the dark.
Ichabod: They are divided.

Ichabod: What is appropriate material for an inventor to wear?
Eutychus: Search me.
Ichabod: Patent leather.

Ichabod: What is the difference between a sewing machine and a kiss?
Eutychus: You've got me guessing.
Ichabod: One sews seams nice, the other seems so nice.

30

Levi: What grows larger the more you take away?
Lois: Beats me.
Levi: A hole.

Levi: How can you change a pumpkin into another vegetable?
Lois: I can't guess.
Levi: Throw it down onto the ground and it will become squash.

Levi: Why did Mr. and Mrs. Cat get married?
Lois: I have no clue.
Levi: They were a purrfect match.

Levi: Why didn't Clara like the joke about the Grand Canyon?
Lois: I don't know.
Levi: It was too deep.

Levi: What do sharks eat with their peanut butter?
Lois: I don't have the foggiest.
Levi: Jellyfish.

Levi: What bear never bathes?
Lois: I have no idea.
Levi: Winnie-the-Phew.

Levi: What cow jumps off buildings for fun?
Lois: You tell me.
Levi: A dairy devil.

Levi: What would you get if you crossed a dentist with a military officer?
Lois: I give up.
Levi: A drill sergeant.

Levi: What cowboy never said a word?
Lois: Who knows?
Levi: Quiet Earp.

Levi: What do you get from a forgetful cow?
Lois: You've got me.
Levi: Milk of Amnesia.

Levi: What do you get from a funny cow?
Lois: My mind is a blank.
Levi: Cream of wit.

Levi: What happened to Little Bo Peep after she spent all day looking for her sheep?
Lois: That's a mystery.
Levi: She was Little Bo Pooped.

Levi: What snowstorm covered the Emerald City?
Lois: Tell me.
Levi: The Blizzard of Oz.

Levi: What do you get when you cross a sheep with a monkey?
Lois: It's unknown to me.
Levi: A baa-boon.

Levi: What's the name of the world's best-known waterfall?
Lois: I'm in the dark.
Levi: Rain.

Levi: What happens to spoons when they work too hard?
Lois: Search me.
Levi: They go stir crazy!

Levi: What has three feet but no toes?
Lois: Beats me.
Levi: A yardstick.

Levi: What has arms but no hands?
Lois: I can't guess.
Levi: A chair.

Levi: Why did the secret agent take two aspirins and go to bed?
Lois: I don't know.
Levi: He had a code in his head.

Levi: What happened when the musician died?
Lois: You've got me guessing.
Levi: He decomposed.

Levi: What did Bambi put on the back of his car?
Lois: I have no idea.
Levi: A Thumper sticker.

Levi: What does a veterinarian keep outside his front door?
Lois: You tell me.
Levi: A welcome mutt.

Levi: What do you have in December that you don't have in any other month?
Lois: I give up.
Levi: The letter D.

Levi: What do jigsaw puzzles do when they get bad news?
Lois: Who knows?
Levi: Go to pieces.

Levi: What do you call a pair of salesmen who go to jail?
Lois: You've got me.
Levi: Sell-mates.

Levi: What happens when you fall in love with a jogger?
Lois: That's a mystery.
Levi: You get the run-around.

Levi: What would you call a bird who joins the Ice Capades?
Lois: Tell me.
Levi: A cheep skate.

Levi: Why do we need the reindeer?
Lois: I don't have the foggiest.
Levi: It makes the little flowers grow.

Levi: Why did the secret agent whisper one, two, three, four, five, six, seven?
Lois: It's unknown to me.
Levi: He was a counter-spy.

Levi: What state doesn't feel good?
Lois: I'm in the dark.
Levi: Ill.

Levi: What grows on a tree and is terrified of wolves?
Lois: Search me.
Levi: The Three Little Figs.

Levi: Do you know how long cows should be milked?
Lois: Beats me.
Levi: The same as short cows.

Levi: How does a dentist examine a crocodile's teeth?
Lois: I can't guess.
Levi: Very carefully!

Levi: Why did the carpenter hire a secretary?
Lois: I don't know.
Levi: To file his nails.

Levi: What do you call a sheep who hangs out with 40 thieves?
Lois: I have no idea.
Levi: Ali Baa Baa.

Levi: What's the easiest job in the world?
Lois: I give up.
Levi: The head of the Crazy Intelligence Agency.

Levi: What kills crazy flies by sitting on them?
Lois: My mind is a blank.
Levi: A fly squatter.

Levi: Why wouldn't the lightning bolt go to the storm?
Lois: I have no idea.
Levi: Because it was on strike.

Levi: What happens to a dog who eats table scraps?
Lois: You've got me.
Levi: He gets splinters in his tongue.

Levi: What is purple and a member of your family?
Lois: That's a mystery.
Levi: Your grape grandmother.

Levi: What did the cat say when his tail got caught in the lawnmower?
Lois: Tell me.
Levi: It won't be long now.

Levi: What did the stocking say to the needle?
Lois: I'm in the dark.
Levi: I'll be darned!

Levi: What did Jonah say when asked how he was feeling?
Lois: Search me.
Levi: Very whale, thank you.

Levi: Why were 1980, 1984, and 1988 good years for kangaroos?
Lois: I have no clue.
Levi: They were leap years.

Levi: Why did the farmer's horse go over the mountain?
Lois: I don't know.
Levi: He couldn't go under it.

Levi: Why does a watermelon contain so much water?
Lois: Beats me.
Levi: It was planted in the spring.

Levi: Why did the man have to go to the hospital after a tomato fell on his head?
Lois: You tell me.
Levi: It was in a can.

Levi: Why do elephants have ivory tusks?
Lois: I can't guess.
Levi: Iron ones would rust.

Levi: Why does a dog wag his tail?
Lois: I have no idea.
Levi: Nobody will wag it for him.

Levi: Why did the boy stand behind the donkey?
Lois: I give up.
Levi: He thought he would get a kick out of it.

Levi: Why don't elephants play basketball?
Lois: Who knows?
Levi: They can't buy round sneakers.

Levi: Why did the farmer feed his sheep chunks of steel?
Lois: You've got me.
Levi: He wanted them to grow steel wool.

Levi: Why are wolves like cards?
Lois: That's a mystery.
Levi: They come in packs.

Levi: Why do giraffes have such long necks?
Lois: I'm a blank.
Levi: To connect their heads to their bodies.

Levi: Why couldn't the pony talk?
Lois: I don't have the foggiest.
Levi: He was a little horse.

Levi: Why are leopards spotted?
Lois: It's unknown to me.
Levi: So you can tell them from fleas.

Levi: Why did Santa have only seven reindeer on Christmas Eve?
Lois: I'm in the dark.
Levi: Comet was home cleaning the sink.

Levi: Why does the joker go to bed with 50 cents every night?
Lois: I pass.
Levi: They're his sleeping quarters.

Levi: Why doesn't the joker use mothballs to get rid of moths?
Lois: I don't know.
Levi: He can't aim those tiny mothballs to hit the moths.

Levi: Why did the joker brush his teeth with gunpowder?
Lois: I have no clue.
Levi: He wanted to shoot his mouth off.

First cowboy: He's a real tough hombre. Quick on the trigger too. His guns are blazing before they clear the holster.
Second cowboy: What's his name?
First cowboy: No-Toes Smith.

Judge: Why did you hit your dentist?
Man: Because he got on my nerves.

Girl: Would you love me just the same if my father lost all his money?
Boy: He hasn't lost it, has he?
Girl: No.
Boy: Of course I would, you silly girl.

Little boy (calling father at office): Hello, who is this?
Father (recognizing his son's voice): The smartest man in the world.
Little boy: Pardon me, I got the wrong number.

Ella: Would you rather have an elephant chase you or a lion?
Reginald: I would rather have the elephant chase the lion.

Norris: Well, how are you getting on in your new ten-room house?
Owen: Oh, not so badly. We furnished one of the bedrooms by collecting soap coupons.
Norris: Didn't you furnish the other nine rooms?
Owen: We can't. They're full of soap.

Mama Owl: I'm worried about Junior.
Papa Owl: What's the matter?
Mama Owl: He just doesn't give a hoot about anything.

Harry: My big brother shaves every day.
Larry: That's nothing! Mine shaves 50 times a day.
Harry: He must be crazy.
Larry: No, he's a barber.

32

I have one teacher who is so forgetful he gave the same test three weeks in a row. If he does that two more times, I may pass it.

Student 1: My teacher thinks I'm a perfect idiot.
Student 2: Well, she is wrong. Nobody is perfect.

Teacher: How long did Thomas Edison live?
Student: All his life.

Teacher: You got a perfect zero on your exam. How did you do that?
Student: It was luck. I guessed at some of the answers.

You can always spot an abnormal student. He is the one who comes back to school from a long vacation and remembers to bring his homework.

Teacher: Who can tell us something about Good Friday?
Student: He was the fellow who helped Robinson Crusoe.

Teacher: Clay, what is the definition of ignorance?
Clay: I don't know.

Teacher: When did Napoleon die?
Student: Die? I didn't even know he was sick.

Teacher: What do you expect to be when you get out of school?
Student: An old man.

Teacher: There will be an eclipse of the moon tonight. Perhaps your parents will let you stay up and watch it.
Student: What channel?

Teacher: Where's Moscow?
Student: In the barn beside pa's cow.

Teacher: Donald, can you give me one use for a horse hide?
Donald: Well, I guess it helps to hold the horse together.

Teacher: If you were dying, where would you go?
Student: To the living room.

Teacher: Are you any good at arithmetic?
Student: Yes and no.
Teacher: What does that mean?
Student: Yes, I'm no good at arithmetic.

Teacher: John, do you know anything about this broken window?
John: Well, sort of...
Teacher: What happened?
John: I was cleaning my slingshot, and it went off accidentally.

Teacher: I asked you to write an essay on cheese last night for your homework. Where is it?
Student: I tried, but the cheese kept blocking up the tip of my pen.

Principal: Now, Amanda, did you really call your teacher a meany?
Amanda: Yes, I did.
Principal: And is it true you called her a wicked old witch?
Amanda: Yes, it is.
Principal: And did you call her a tomato-nosed beanbag?
Amanda: No, but I'll remember that one for next time!

Teacher: How do you spell Mississippi?
Willie: The state or the river?

Teacher: If I give you five goldfish today and seven goldfish tomorrow, how many will you have?
Susie: Fourteen.
Teacher: How do you figure that?
Susie: I already have two goldfish.

Teacher: How many feet are there in a yard?
Student: Well, it depends on how many people there are.

One kid in our class has never missed or been late with one single homework assignment. The rest of the class was so proud of him that we chipped in and bought him a television set.

Teacher: How is your little brother, John?
John: Sick in bed. He hurt himself.
Teacher: That's too bad. How did he do it?
John: We were playing who could lean farthest out the window and he won.

Did you hear about the absentminded professor? He returned from lunch and saw a sign on the door, "Back in 30 minutes," and sat down and waited for himself.

Teacher: Give me a sentence with an object.
Student: You're very beautiful, teacher.
Teacher: What is the object?
Student: A good grade.

Teacher: There will be only a half day of school this morning.
Pupils: Whoopee! Hooray!
Teacher: We'll have the other half this afternoon.

Teacher: Frankie, give me a sentence with the word "Camelot" in it.
Student: Right, teacher. A camelot is a place where the Arabs park their camels!

"The principal thinks I am very responsible," the boy told his mother. "Every time something goes wrong at school, he says I am responsible."

I have the toughest teacher in the world. In most classes you bring an apple for the teacher. With this teacher you bring raw meat.

Teacher: This is the fifth day this week you're late! What do you have to say for yourself?
Student: I'm sure glad it's Friday.

Teacher: If you had five pieces of candy, and Joey asked you for one, how many pieces would you have left?
Student: Five.

Student: I don't have a pencil to take this exam.
Teacher: What would you think of a soldier who went into battle without a gun?
Student: I'd think he was an officer.

Teacher: Name four animals that belong to the cat family.
Student: The mama cat, the papa cat, and two kittens.

A teacher sent this note home to the parents of one of her pupils: "Lester is trying—very."

Teacher: If you insist on talking, I'll have to send you to the principal's office.
Student: Oh, does the principal want somebody to talk to?

Principal: Are there any unusual children in your class?
Teacher: Yes, three of them have good manners.

Teacher: Birds, though small, are remarkable creatures. For example, what can a bird do that I can't?
Student: Take a bath in a saucer.

Teacher: If I lay one egg on this chair and two on the table, how many will I have altogether?
Student: Personally, I don't believe you can do it.

Teacher: If you had three apples and ate one, how many would you have?
Student: Three.
Teacher: Three?
Student: Yes. Two outside and one inside.

Teacher: Did you reprimand your little boy for mimicking me?
Parent: Yes, I told him not to act like a fool.

Teacher: A job well done need not be done again.
Student: What about mowing the lawn?

Teacher: If I had ten oranges in one hand and six in the other, what would I have?
Student: Big hands.

Teacher: Tell me about the Iron Age.
Student: Sorry, I'm a little rusty on that subject.

33

Show me a guy who plays basketball in a tuxedo,
and I'll show you a gym dandy.

Show me a swine, and I'll show you hogwash.

Show me a burned-out post office, and I'll
show you a case of blackmail.

Show me where Stalin is buried, and I'll show you a Communist plot.

Show me a cross between a cannon and a bell,
and I'll show you a boomerang.

Show me a toddler caught playing in the mud, and
I'll show you grime and punishment.

Show me a stolen sausage, and I'll show you a missing link.

Show me a gang of beggars, and I'll show you a ragtime band.

Show me a man who's afraid of Christmas,
and I'll show you a Noel Coward.

Show me a frog on a lily pad, and I'll show you a toadstool.

Show me an arrogant insect, and I'll show you a cocky roach.

Show me a man convicted of two crimes, and
I'll show you a compound sentence.

Show me the first president's dentures, and I'll show
you the George Washington bridge.

Show me a squirrel's nest, and I'll show you the Nutcracker Suite.

Show me a cat that just ate a lemon, and I'll show you a sourpuss.

Show me a pharaoh who ate crackers in bed, and
I'll show you a crumby mummy.

Show me Santa's helpers, and I'll show you subordinate clauses.

34

Cyrus: What was the turtle doing on the freeway?
Cornelia: I have no clue.
Cyrus: About half a mile an hour.

Cyrus: What kind of hawk has no wings?
Cornelia: I don't know.
Cyrus: A tomahawk.

Cyrus: What did the pelican say when he caught a large fish?
Cornelia: Beats me.
Cyrus: This sure fills the bill.

Cyrus: What do you get if you cross a potato with an onion?
Cornelia: You tell me.
Cyrus: A potato with watery eyes.

Cyrus: What should you do with a dog who is eating a dictionary?
Cornelia: My mind is a blank.
Cyrus: Take the words right out of his mouth.

Cyrus: What sort of story did the peacock tell?
Cornelia: I can't guess.
Cyrus: A big tale.

Cyrus: What animal is a tattletale?
Cornelia: I give up.
Cyrus: The pig always squeals on you.

Cyrus: What is green, then purple, then green, then purple?
Cornelia: Who knows?
Cyrus: A pickle that works part-time as a grape.

Cyrus: What animal is the best baseball player?
Cornelia: You've got me.
Cyrus: The bat.

Cyrus: What is a monkey that eats potato chips called?
Cornelia: That's a mystery.
Cyrus: A chip monk.

Cyrus: What would you get if you crossed a porcupine and a skunk?
Cornelia: I'm a blank.
Cyrus: A smelly pincushion.

Cyrus: What must a lion tamer know to teach a lion tricks?
Cornelia: I don't have the foggiest.
Cyrus: More than the lion.

Cyrus: What did the beaver say to the tree?
Cornelia: It's unknown to me.
Cyrus: It's been nice gnawing you.

Cyrus: What do hippopotamuses have that no other animals have?
Cornelia: I'm in the dark.
Cyrus: Baby hippos.

Cyrus: What makes more noise than an angry lion?
Cornelia: Search me.
Cyrus: Two angry lions.

Cyrus: What is the highest form of animal life?
Cornelia: I don't know.
Cyrus: A giraffe.

Cyrus: What should you do if you find a gorilla asleep in your bed?
Cornelia: I have no clue.
Cyrus: Sleep somewhere else.

Cyrus: What is an important aid in good grooming for pet mice?
Cornelia: I have no clue.
Cyrus: Mouse wash.

Cyrus: What did the mama broom and the papa broom say to the baby broom?
Cornelia: I don't know.
Cyrus: Go to sweep.

Cyrus: What do you get when you cross a camel with the town dump?
Cornelia: Beats me.
Cyrus: Humpty-Dumpty.

Cyrus: What fish is man's best friend?
Cornelia: You tell me.
Cyrus: The dogfish.

Cyrus: What beans won't grow from seeds?
Cornelia: My mind is a blank.
Cyrus: Jelly beans.

Cyrus: What fish goes boating?
Cornelia: I can't guess.
Cyrus: A sailfish.

Cyrus: What do teenage boy gorillas do when they see pretty teenage girl gorillas?
Cornelia: I have no idea.
Cyrus: They go ape.

Cyrus: What kind of dog can fly?
Cornelia: I give up.
Cyrus: A bird dog.

Cyrus: What animal eats with its tail?
Cornelia: Who knows?
Cyrus: All animals do. They also sleep with them.

Cyrus: What is gray, has four legs, and weighs 98 pounds?
Cornelia: You've got me.
Cyrus: A fat mouse.

Cyrus: What do you call a meeting among many dogs?
Cornelia: I don't have the foggiest.
Cyrus: A bowwow powwow.

Cyrus: What do dogs always take on their camping trips?
Cornelia: It's unknown to me.
Cyrus: Pup tents.

Cyrus: What was the first cat to fly?
Cornelia: I pass.
Cyrus: Kitty Hawk.

Cyrus: What did the joker get when he crossed poison ivy with a four-leaf clover?
Cornelia: I don't know.
Cyrus: A rash of good luck.

Cyrus: What would you get if you crossed a cat and a pair of galoshes?
Cornelia: I have no clue.
Cyrus: Puss 'n' boots.

Cyrus: What is yellow and always points north?
Cornelia: Beats me.
Cyrus: A magnetic banana.

Abner: What's red and white and blue all over?
Abigail: I don't know.
Abner: A candy cane holding its breath!

Abner: What do you get if you cross a rattlesnake with a doughnut?
Abigail: Beats me.
Abner: A snake that rattles and rolls.

Abner: What country do cows love to visit?
Abigail: I can't guess.
Abner: Moo Zealand!

Abner: What do you get if you cross a lizard with a baseball player?
Abigail: I have no idea.
Abner: An outfielder who catches flies on his tongue and eats them.

Abner: What do you feed your pet frog?
Abigail: My mind is blank.
Abner: Croakers and milk!

Abner: What always has its eye open but never sees anything?
Abigail: That's a mystery.
Abner: A needle.

Abner: What's so fragile you can break it with a whisper?
Abigail: It's unknown to me.
Abner: A secret.

Abner: What's the difference between a dog and a hockey puck?
Abigail: I'm blank.
Abner: About two IQ points.

Abner: What can fill a whole house and still weigh less than a tiny mouse?
Abigail: I'm in the dark.
Abner: Smoke.

Abner: What did one pig say to another?
Abigail: You've got me guessing.
Abner: I'll give you lots of hogs and kisses.

Abner: What would you get if you crossed Prince Charles with Moby Dick?
Abigail: How should I know?
Abner: The Prince of Whales.

Abner: How can you stop a dog from barking in the backyard?
Abigail: Beats me.
Abner: Put him in the front yard.

Abner: How do you get fur from a bear?
Abigail: You tell me.
Abner: Run fast in the opposite direction.

Abner: How do you move in a crowd of porcupines?
Abigail: My mind is a blank.
Abner: Very carefully.

Abner: How did the joker make a hotdog shiver?
Abigail: I can't guess.
Abner: He covered it with chili beans.

Abner: How does the joker file an ax?
Abigail: I have no idea.
Abner: Under the letter A.

Abner: How did the joker eat a computer?
Abigail: I give up.
Abner: Bit by bit.

Abner: How does the joker make a banana split?
Abigail: Who knows?
Abner: He cuts it in half.

Abner: How did the joker fit a rhinoceros into his car?
Abigail: You've got me.
Abner: He made one of the elephants get out.

Abner: What song does the mean man sing at Christmastime?
Abigail: I have no clue.
Abner: "Deck the halls with poison ivy, fa la la la la..."

Abner: What does the computer eat for lunch?
Abigail: I don't know.
Abner: Floppy Joes and microchips.

Abner: What would you get if you crossed a puppy with a mean boy?
Abigail: Beats me.
Abner: A bully dog.

Abner: What would you get if you crossed a pit bull and a cow?
Abigail: You tell me.
Abner: An animal that's too mean to milk.

Abner: What did the joker get when he put his dog in the bathtub?
Abigail: My mind is a blank.
Abner: Ring around the collie.

Abner: What does the joker call a man who shaves 20 times a day?
Abigail: I can't guess.
Abner: A barber.

Abner: What happened when the joker robbed the hamburger factory?
Abigail: I give up.
Abner: Things came to a grinding halt.

Abner: What goes A B C D E F G H I J K L M N O P Q R S T U V W X Y Z slurp?
Abigail: Who knows?
Abner: A boy eating a bowl of alphabet soup.

Abner: What's black and white and goes around and around?
Abigail: You've got me.
Abner: A penguin in a revolving door.

Abner: What did the boy get when he crossed a string quartet with a chocolate dessert?
Abigail: That's a mystery.
Abner: Cello pudding.

Abner: What do you call a man who bites a policeman?
Abigail: I'm a blank.
Abner: A law a-biting citizen.

Abner: What did the man get when he crossed some cabbage with a tiger?
Abigail: I don't have the foggiest.
Abner: Man-eating coleslaw.

Abner: What kind of a waiter never accepts a tip?
Abigail: I'm in the dark.
Abner: A dumbwaiter.

Abner: What's black and white and hides in a cave?
Abigail: Search me.
Abner: A zebra that owes money.

Abner: What kind of water can't be frozen?
Abigail: I pass.
Abner: Boiling water.

Abner: What did the man get when he dialed 555-2738593613943647 37 on his cell phone?
Abigail: I don't know.
Abner: A blister on his finger.

Abner: What does the joker fill his car with?
Abigail: I have no clue.
Abner: Laughing gas.

36

What did the sailor say?
Knot bad.

What did the drummer say?
It's hard to beat.

What did the coffee salesperson say?
It's a grind.

What did the demolition worker say?
Smashing!

What did the dressmaker say?
Just sew-sew.

What did the astronomer say?
Things are looking up.

What did the street cleaner say?
Things are picking up.

What did the botanist say?
Everything's coming up roses.

What did the pianist say?
Right on key.

What did the deep-sea diver say?
I'm about to go under.

What did the floor waxer say?
Going smoothly.

What did the zookeeper say?
It's beastly!

What did the teacher say?
My work is classy.

What did the gravedigger say?
Monumental!

What did the iceman say?
Not so hot.

What did the counterfeiter say?
We're forging on.

What did the dairy farmer say?
Cheesy, in a whey.

What did the baker say?
I've been making a lot of dough lately.

What did the tree surgeon say?
I've some shady deals going.

What did the pilot say?
Pretty much up in the air.

What did the photographer say?
Everything is clicking and developing well.

What did the locksmith say?
Everything's opening up.

What did the musician say?
Nothing of note has been happening.

37

"Come, come, come," said one who was wide-awake to one who was fast asleep. "Get up, get up! Don't you know it's the early bird that catches the worm?"

"Serves the worm right," said the grumbling sleeper. "Worms shouldn't get up before the birds do."

Roses are red;
Violets are blue;
I copied your paper,
And I flunked too.

A lady purchased a postage stamp at the post office. "Must I stick it on myself?" she asked.

"No, madam," replied the postal clerk. "It would be better if you stuck it on the envelope."

"Is she Hungary?" Wilbur asked.

"Alaska," said Wesley.

"Yes, Siam," she replied.

"All right. I'll Fiji," Wilbur offered.

"Oh, don't Russia," Wesley admonished.

"What if she Wales?" Wilbur demanded.

"Give her a Canada Chile," Wesley suggested.

"I'd rather have Turkey," she said. "Except that I can't have any Greece."

When the waiter brought the check, Wilbur asked Wesley, "Look and see how much Egypt you."

Three boys were talking.

"I have my father's nose and my mother's eyes," said the first boy.

"I have my grandfather's forehead and my uncle's ears," said the second boy.

"I have my brother's pants," piped up the third.

A man called on the director of a television show. He was carrying a sledgehammer, a huge rock, and a large paper sack.

"In my act, I put this rock on my head, and my assistant breaks it with this sledgehammer. I take a bow and then walk off the stage."

"Well, what do you have in the paper sack?" asked the director.

"Aspirin," the man said.

If you had a box of candles and matches, how would you make it weigh less?

Take one out and it will be a candle lighter.

Two leopards in the zoo had just finished lunch. One sat back against the bars and said, "Mm-mm-mm! That really hit the spots."

I just couldn't get good grades in masonry school. Studying was like banging my head against a brick wall.

A young man who just joined the army wrote his mother the following letter: "Dear Mom: For the last 21 years you have been trying to teach me to clean my room, hang up my clothes, eat good food, go to bed early, and shine my shoes. Well, the army has taught me to do the whole thing in one week. Love, Quentin."

Two kids were talking one day.

The first boy said, "I have to get a calendar."

The other boy asked, "Why?"

The first boy answered, "Because yesterday I got sick so I wouldn't have to go to school, and then I found out it was Saturday."

The young couple couldn't wait to get married. They got the preacher out of bed at three in the morning to do the job.

The next day a headline in the paper announced, "Preacher Ties Knot in His Pajamas."

Two termites were going out for dinner.

"Let's go eat a house," said the first.

"No, let's eat a pagoda," said the second.

"No good," said the first. "You know how it is with Chinese food. You're hungry again an hour after you eat it."

A grocer leaned over the counter and yelled at a boy who stood close to an apple barrel: "Are you trying to steal those apples, boy?"

"No…no, sir," the boy faltered. "I'm trying not to."

Two fathers were bragging about their children. "My daughter is brilliant," said the first father. "She was able to get her B.A. in only three years."

"That's nothing," said the other. "My daughter got a Ph.D. in only one year."

"That's impossible," said the first man. "How could she get a Ph.D. in one year?"

"She married him," his friend said.

I am the center of gravity.
I am the capital of Vienna.
I am in every victory.
I am in valuable.
I can be seen in the midst of the river.
I could name three who are in love with me.
I have been in the grave.
I have been in heaven.
Still you look in vain to find me.
Who am I?
The letter V.

If a goat should swallow a rabbit, what would be the result?
A hare in the butter.

I once prayed in a hotel and they charged me a 75-cent long distance charge.

We were losing one game 76 to 0, but we weren't worried. We hadn't had our turn at bat yet.

They asked my Uncle Ambrose if anybody in his family suffers from insanity. He said, "No, they all seem to be enjoying it."

Love makes the world go 'round, but laughter keeps us all from jumping off.

We had such a bad team that every time we took the field our manager got fined for littering.

I hate housework. You make the beds, you do the dishes, and six months later you have to start all over again.

Three little boys were bragging about how tough they were.
"I wear out a pair of shoes in a month," the first little boy said.
"I wear out a pair of jeans in a week," the second little boy said.
"That's nothing," the other little boy said. "I wear out a babysitter in 20 minutes."

Today's cars are aerodynamically designed. They're built to sit in traffic jams at high speed.

The teacher in the school for pigeons had just about given up on one of her pupils. "Either you fly tomorrow or I'll put a rope on you and tow you around," she said.

"Oh, don't do that," he said, "I don't want to be pigeon-toed."

39

Jon-Mark: What has fingers and thumbs but no arms?
Malcolm: I don't know.
Jon-Mark: Gloves.

Jon-Mark: What is a good way to keep a dog off the street?
Malcolm: I can't guess.
Jon-Mark: Put him in a barking lot.

Jon-Mark: What's red and eats rocks?
Malcolm: I have no idea.
Jon-Mark: A big red rock eater.

Jon-Mark: What is a fish of precious metal?
Malcolm: You tell me.
Jon-Mark: Goldfish.

Jon-Mark: What fish is a household pet?
Malcolm: I give up.
Jon-Mark: Catfish.

Jon-Mark: What fish is seen at night?
Malcolm: Who knows?
Jon-Mark: Starfish.

Jon-Mark: What fish warms the earth?
Malcolm: You've got me.
Jon-Mark: Sunfish.

Jon-Mark: What do ghosts have for dessert?
Malcolm: My mind's a blank.
Jon-Mark: Booberry pie.

Jon-Mark: What do you get if a sheep studies karate?
Malcolm: I'm blank.
Jon-Mark: A lamb chop.

Jon-Mark: What wears shoes but has no feet?
Malcolm: I don't have the foggiest.
Jon-Mark: The pavement.

Jon-Mark: What do you call a man who lives on a back street?
Malcolm: It's unknown to me.
Jon-Mark: Ali.

Jon-Mark: What do you get if you cross poison ivy with a black cat?
Malcolm: I'm in the dark.
Jon-Mark: A rash of bad luck!

Jon-Mark: What do you call a man who goes fishing?
Malcolm: Search me.
Jon-Mark: Rod.

Jon-Mark: What does the winner of a race lose?
Malcolm: I pass.
Jon-Mark: His breath.

Jon-Mark: What are white and furry and ride horses?
Malcolm: I don't know.
Jon-Mark: Polo bears.

Jon-Mark: What do you call a rabbit with a lot of fleas?
Malcolm: I have no clue.
Jon-Mark: Bugs Bunny!

Jon-Mark: What do you do with a blue whale?
Malcolm: I don't know.
Jon-Mark: Cheer him up.

Jon-Mark: What ocean animals go to Hollywood?
Malcolm: I can't guess.
Jon-Mark: Starfish.

Jon-Mark: What do you call an orange playing a trombone?
Malcolm: I have no idea.
Jon-Mark: A tutti frutti!

Jon-Mark: What letters are most like a Roman emperor?
Malcolm: You tell me.
Jon-Mark: The C's are.

Jon-Mark: What letters are invisible, but never out of sight?
Malcolm: Who knows?
Jon-Mark: I and S.

Jon-Mark: What did the big rose say to the little rose?
Malcolm: You've got me.
Jon-Mark: Hi ya, Bud.

Jon-Mark: What is the difference between an oak tree and a tight shoe?
Malcolm: My mind is blank.
Jon-Mark: One makes acorns, the other makes corns ache.

Jon-Mark: What is the best name for the wife of a gardener?
Malcolm: That's a mystery.
Jon-Mark: Flora.

Jon-Mark: What is the best thing to put into a dish of ice cream?
Malcolm: I don't have the foggiest.
Jon-Mark: A spoon.

Jon-Mark: What has two heads, one tail, four legs on one side, and two legs on the other?
Malcolm: It's unknown to me.
Jon-Mark: A horse with a lady riding sidesaddle.

Jon-Mark: What driver does not need a license?
Malcolm: I'm blank.
Jon-Mark: A screwdriver.

Jon-Mark: What kind of beans grow in a candy garden?
Malcolm: I'm in the dark.
Jon-Mark: Jelly beans.

Jon-Mark: What is the price of the moon?
Malcolm: Search me.
Jon-Mark: Four quarters.

Jon-Mark: What is appropriate material for an artist to wear?
Malcolm: How should I know?
Jon-Mark: Canvas.

Jon-Mark: What animal keeps the best time?
Malcolm: I don't know.
Jon-Mark: A watchdog.

Jon-Mark: What's red and goes putt-putt?
Malcolm: I have no idea.
Jon-Mark: An outboard apple.

Jon-Mark: What do you call the time of prehistoric pigs?
Malcolm: I have no clue.
Jon-Mark: Jurassic Pork.

Jon-Mark: What do you use when a tree has a flat?
Malcolm: I don't know.
Jon-Mark: A lumberjack.

Jon-Mark: What goes boom, squish, boom, squish, boom, squish?
Malcolm: Beats me.
Jon-Mark: An elephant with wet sneakers.

Jon-Mark: What kind of bird always sounds cheerful?
Malcolm: I can't guess.
Jon-Mark: A hummingbird.

Jon-Mark: What kind of snack does a crazy millionaire resemble?
Malcolm: You tell me.
Jon-Mark: A doughnut.

Jon-Mark: What kind of dog works at the United Nations?
Malcolm: I give up.
Jon-Mark: A diplomutt!

Jon-Mark: What is appropriate material for a fat man to wear?
Malcolm: Who knows?
Jon-Mark: Broadcloth.

Jon-Mark: What's pigskin used for mostly?
Malcolm: You've got me.
Jon-Mark: To hold pigs together.

Jon-Mark: What's an astronaut sandwich made of?
Malcolm: My mind is a blank.
Jon-Mark: Launch meat.

Jon-Mark: What do you get when you cross a dinosaur and a skunk?
Malcolm: That's a mystery.
Jon-Mark: A really big stinker.

Jon-Mark: What do you get when you cross a cat with a hyena?
Malcolm: I don't have the foggiest.
Jon-Mark: Gigglepuss.

Jon-Mark: What is the sound of a bee laughing its head off?
Malcolm: It's unknown to me.
Jon-Mark: Buzz. Buzz. Buzz. Plop.

Jon-Mark: What do you get if you cross an elephant with a spider?
Malcolm: I'm blank.
Jon-Mark: I don't know, but when it crawls on your ceiling, the roof collapses!

Jon-Mark: What do you call a cat that likes to dig at the beach?
Malcolm: I'm in the dark.
Jon-Mark: Sandy Claws!

Jon-Mark: What should a runner eat before a race?
Malcolm: Search me.
Jon-Mark: Ketchup.

Jon-Mark: What did the hummingbird say when it laid an ostrich egg?
Malcolm: You've got me guessing.
Jon-Mark: Ouch!

Jon-Mark: What is the hardest thing about learning to ride a bike?
Malcolm: How should I know?
Jon-Mark: The sidewalk.

Jon-Mark: What kind of dial should you not get too close to?
Malcolm: Beats me.
Jon-Mark: A crocodile.

40

Ivan: What is the best way to kill time?
Isabel: I can't guess.
Ivan: Work it to death.

Ivan: Why was the calendar so sad?
Isabel: I have no clue.
Ivan: It's days were numbered.

Ivan: Why was the duck unhappy?
Isabel: I don't know.
Ivan: His bill was in the mail.

Ivan: What is a frog asked when it enters a restaurant?
Isabel: I have no idea.
Ivan: Croaking or noncroaking?

Ivan: What can you hold without touching it?
Isabel: Beats me.
Ivan: Your breath.

Ivan: What kind of house weighs the least?
Isabel: You tell me.
Ivan: A lighthouse.

Ivan: What is green, red, orange, yellow, purple, brown, pink, and covered with polka dots?
Isabel: I give up.
Ivan: A crazy woman dressed up for church.

Ivan: What does it say on the bottom of Coke bottles in Crazyland?
Isabel: Who knows?
Ivan: Open other end.

Ivan: What time is it when 12 dogs chase a cat?
Isabel: My mind is a blank.
Ivan: Twelve after one.

Ivan: What do mechanics do in aerobics class?
Isabel: That's a mystery.
Ivan: Touch their tow trucks.

Ivan: What turkey starred in *Gone with the Wind?*
Isabel: I don't have the foggiest.
Ivan: Clark Gobble.

Ivan: What was Chicken Superman's other name?
Isabel: It's unknown to me.
Ivan: Cluck Kent.

Ivan: What is worse than a turtle with claustrophobia?
Isabel: I'm in the dark.
Ivan: An elephant with hay fever.

Ivan: What practical jokes do mathematicians play?
Isabel: Search me.
Ivan: Arithmetricks.

Ivan: What can you tell me about the great chemists of the seventeenth century?
Isabel: I have no clue.
Ivan: They are all dead.

Ivan: What town doesn't have crime in the streets?
Isabel: Beats me.
Ivan: Venice.

Ivan: What did one flea say to the other flea?
Isabel: I can't guess.
Ivan: Shall we walk or shall we take the dog?

Ivan: What do you call the place where they shear sheep?
Isabel: I have no idea.
Ivan: A baa-baa shop.

Ivan: What is a nerve specialist?
Isabel: You tell me.
Ivan: A tic doc!

Ivan: What is yellow, soft, and goes round and round?
Isabel: I give up.
Ivan: A long-playing omelette.

Ivan: What is the difference between a home, a sigh, and a donkey?
Isabel: Who knows?
Ivan: A home is so dear, a sigh is oh, dear, and a donkey is you, dear.

Ivan: What do you give to an old lady just passing 65?
Isabel: You've got me.
Ivan: A traffic ticket.

Ivan: What could you call the small rivers that flow into the Nile?
Isabel: My mind's a blank.
Ivan: Juveniles.

Ivan: What is the difference between a coat and a baby?
Isabel: That's a mystery.
Ivan: One you wear and the other you were.

Ivan: What do you call a sunburn on your stomach?
Isabel: I'm blank.
Ivan: Pot roast.

Ivan: What is a haunted wigwam?
Isabel: Search me.
Ivan: A creepy tepee.

Ivan: What is a ghoul's favorite food for lunch?
Isabel: I pass.
Ivan: Goulash.

Ivan: What room do you bounce around in?
Isabel: How should I know?
Ivan: A ballroom.

Ivan: What is a tiny laugh in Indian language?
Isabel: I have no clue.
Ivan: A Minnehaha.

Ivan: What kind of artist can't you trust?
Isabel: I don't know.
Ivan: A sculptor, because he is always chiseling.

Ivan: What is the difference between a farmer and a dressmaker?
Isabel: Beats me.
Ivan: A farmer gathers what he sows, and a dressmaker sews what she gathers.

Ivan: What is very light but can't be lifted?
Isabel: I can't guess.
Ivan: A bubble.

Ivan: What do you call a boomerang that doesn't come back?
Isabel: I have no clue.
Ivan: A stick.

Ivan: What is appropriate material for a dairyman to wear?
Isabel: I don't know.
Ivan: Cheesecloth.

Ivan: What is the best name for the wife of a civil engineer?
Isabel: Beats me.
Ivan: Bridget.

Ivan: Who was the strongest man in the Bible?
Isabel: I can't guess.
Ivan: Jonah; the whale couldn't keep him down.

Ivan: What beverage is appropriate for a golfer?
Isabel: I have no idea.
Ivan: Tea.

Ivan: What is always coming but never arrives?
Isabel: You tell me.
Ivan: Tomorrow.

Ivan: What letter is nine inches long?
Isabel: I give up.
Ivan: The letter Y; it is one-fourth of a yard.

Ivan: What did one arithmetic book say to the other?
Isabel: Who knows?
Ivan: I've got problems.

Ivan: What did one watch say to another?
Isabel: My mind is blank.
Ivan: Hour you doing?

Ivan: What did one shrub say to the other?
Isabel: That's a mystery.
Ivan: Boy, am I bushed.

Ivan: What is the difference between progress and Congress?
Isabel: I don't have the foggiest.
Ivan: Pro and con.

Ivan: What is the best name for the wife of a jeweler?
Isabel: It's unknown to me.
Ivan: Ruby.

Ivan: What time is it when you see a monkey scratching for fleas with his left hand?
Isabel: I'm blank.
Ivan: Five after one.

Ivan: What is the best name for the wife of a lawyer?
Isabel: I'm in the dark.
Ivan: Sue.

Ivan: What is a good way to kill time in the winter?
Isabel: Search me.
Ivan: Sleigh it.

Ivan: What is big enough to hold a pig and small enough to hold in your hands?
Isabel: I pass.
Ivan: A pen.

Ivan: What is the difference between a cat and a bullfrog?
Isabel: How should I know?
Ivan: The cat has nine lives, but the bullfrog croaks every night.

Ivan: What kind of servants are best for hotels?
Isabel: I don't know.
Ivan: The inn-experienced.

Ivan: What has four legs and flies?
Isabel: I have no idea.
Ivan: A horse.

Ivan: What is the most dangerous animal in the yard?
Isabel: I have no clue.
Ivan: A clotheslion.

Ivan: What is the best name for the wife of a gambler?
Isabel: I don't know.
Ivan: Betty.

Ivan: What suit lasts longer than you want it to?
Isabel: Beats me.
Ivan: A lawsuit.

Ivan: What is the best name for the wife of a doctor?
Isabel: You've got me.
Ivan: Patience.

Ivan: What is appropriate material for a filling-station operator to wear?
Isabel: I'm blank.
Ivan: Oilcloth.

Ivan: Which clothes last the longest?
Isabel: I'm in the dark.
Ivan: Pajamas, for they are never worn out.

Ivan: What has 50 heads but can't think?
Isabel: Search me.
Ivan: A box of matches.

Ivan: What three noblemen are mentioned in the Bible?
Isabel: You've got me guessing.
Ivan: Barren fig tree, Lord how long, and Count thy blessings.

Ivan: What is the sharpest tool mentioned in the Bible?
Isabel: I pass.
Ivan: The Acts of the Apostles.

Ivan: What has a head like a cat, feet like a cat, a tail like a cat, but isn't a cat?
Isabel: How should I know?
Ivan: A kitten.

Ivan: What did Adam first plant in the Garden of Eden?
Isabel: I don't know.
Ivan: His foot.

41

Barbie: I'm engaged to an Irishman.
Laurie: Oh, really?
Barbie: No, O'Reilly.

Mack: Are you a Giant fan?
Jack: Yes.
Mack: Well, I'm a little air conditioner.

Larry: I couldn't sleep last night.
Jerry: Why not?
Larry: I plugged the electric blanket into the toaster by mistake, and I kept popping out of bed all night.

Karl: Did you hear about the skunk who couldn't swim?
Eli: No, what about him?
Karl: He stank to the bottom of the pool.

Teacher: If you stood with your back to the north and faced due south, what would be on your left hand?
Student: Fingers.

Lady: Give me a ticket to Toledo.
Agent: Do you want to go by Buffalo?
Lady: No, I prefer to go by train.

Melody: I was in hot water last night.
Marcy: Why is that?
Melody: I had to take a bath.

Mother: I hear you've been fighting with one of those boys next door and have given him a black eye.
Son: Yes'm. You see, they're twins, and I wanted some way to tell them apart.

Mother: Son, the canary has disappeared.
Son: That's funny. It was there when I cleaned the cage with the vacuum cleaner.

Mother: Auntie will never kiss you with a dirty face.
Son: That's what I thought.

Bill: I wish I had enough money to buy an elephant.
Jill: What in the world do you want an elephant for?
Bill: I don't. I just wish I had that much money.

Nit: What do you call a 200-pound man with a club?
Wit: Sir!

Boy: You need to learn more about baseball. Do you know what RBI stands for?
Girl: Really Boring Information.

Private: I've come to see General Parker.
Sergeant: I'm sorry, but the general is sick today.
Private: What made him sick?
Sergeant: Oh, things in general.

Rex: I went to see my girl last night.
Tex: Did you stay late?
Rex: Well, I guess I did, but I kept turning the clock back and finally my girl's father yelled down from upstairs and said, "That clock has struck 12 three times now—would you mind letting it practice on one for a while?"

Lydia: Where did he meet her?
Lucile: They met in a revolving door, and he's been going around with her ever since.

First sardine: How do you hug a hungry shark?
Second sardine: Very carefully.

Customer: When I bought this cat, you told me he was good for mice. He doesn't go near them.
Clerk: Well, isn't that good for mice?

Bill: What do you do?
Jill: I'm a dairy maid in a candy factory.
Bill: So what do you do?
Jill: I milk chocolates.

Mark: My father has Washington's shoe.
Clark: That's nothing. My father has Adam's apple.

The other day I went to a flea market looking for a bargain. All I came home with was fleas.

A woman went to the store to buy some diapers for her baby. The clerk said, "That will be a dollar plus tax, ma'am."
"I don't use tacks. I use safety pins," the woman replied.

If a telephone and a piece of paper should run a race, which would win?
The telephone because the paper would always remain stationary.

One morning a boy couldn't find his trousers. What did he do?
He raced around the room until he was breathing in short pants.

Have I got a neat neighbor. She's so neat she puts paper under the cuckoo clock.

The good news is my father just doubled my allowance. The bad news is two times zero is zero.

One day Jeremy's father brought his boss home for dinner. When Jeremy's mother served the meat, the little boy asked, "Is this mutton?"

His mother replied, "No. Why do you ask?"

"Because Dad said he was going to bring home a muttonhead for dinner," Jeremy answered.

A room with eight corners had a cat in each corner, seven cats before each cat, and a cat on every cat's tail. How many cats were in the room?

Eight.

I know I'm a lousy cook, but I never realized how bad until the other night when I caught the dog calling Taco Bell.

Our house is such a mess the termites tried to have us exterminated.

If butter is a dollar a pound in Los Angeles, what are windowpanes in New York?

Glass.

It is so simple to be smart. Just think of something stupid to say, and then say the opposite.

Last Christmas my father gave me a bat. First time I tried to play with it, it flew away.

According to an old superstitious belief, the wearing of a ruby would preserve one from injury by falling. A medieval king who wore a ruby ring asked his jester one day: "What do you think would happen if I jumped off the highest part of the castle with this ruby ring on my finger?"

The jester replied with a ready wit worthy of his office, "The ruby, my lord, would probably not be hurt."

I know a guy who owes so much money to so many people his answering machine just says, "Hi, your check's in the mail."

Roses are red;
Pansies are purple;
Drink too much pop
And you're liable to burple.

First hunter: Good heavens. Cannibals.
Second hunter: Now don't get in a stew.

One evening at the neighborhood miniature golf course a man and his wife found themselves following a young couple with a tiny baby. The couple had worked out a system. They would trade the baby back and forth between them after each shot. But progress was very slow.

Finally, the man and wife who were following them became impatient. The lady said, "It seems to me that you should have hired a babysitter."

"Oh," said the girl who was holding the baby at the moment, "we are the babysitters."

A courtship begins when a man whispers sweet nothings, and ends when he says nothing sweet.

First woman: Who is your favorite writer?
Second woman: My husband.
First woman: What does he write?
Second woman: Checks.

"Nathan," said his mother severely, "there were two pieces of cake in the pantry this morning, and now there is only one. How is that?"
"I don't know," replied Nathan regretfully. "It must have been so dark I didn't see the other piece."

Baseball players are getting too rich. They hit the ball now and have their chauffeurs run to first for them.

I once had a dog who really believed he was man's best friend. He kept borrowing money from me.

Rumor has it that tall people live longer lives than short people.

Last week I asked my mom to make Hungarian stew for me, but she couldn't. She said the butcher shop was out of Hungarians.

They call it a family tree because if you look hard enough, you'll always find some nut or sap in it.

I know a guy who is always late for everything. He was three years old at his first birthday party.

Karla had just hit her little brother. Her mother told her, "That was an unladylike thing to do. Ladies don't hit people. They outtalk them."

The first thing a boy learns who has received a chemistry set for Christmas is that he isn't ever going to be given another one.

A father was trying to break up his daughter's habit of making too many telephone calls. In an effort to slow her down he made a small sign for the telephone that read: Is this call really necessary?

The next day he found this sign in its place:

How can I tell until after I have made it?

One friend of mine was so stupid he had to take the IQ test twice to get it up to a whole number.

A song heard by a hive: "Bee it ever so humble, there's no place like comb."

During a Ping Pong game, one of the contestants accidentally swallowed the ball. The ambulance came and rushed him off to the hospital, where he was quickly rushed into the operating room.

When he recovered after the operation, he noticed a dozen scars all over his body, some on his chest, some on his stomach. "Why did you cut me in so many places?" he asked the doctor.

"That's the way the ball bounces," answered the surgeon.

I was a five-letter man my first year in high school and the letters were F-L-U-N-K.

Football is getting rough. You have to wear shoulder pads, a face mask, and a helmet…and that's just to sit in the stands.

It's tough to go through an identity crisis when you're apathetic. You don't know who you are, and you couldn't care less about finding the answer.

I won't say my house is a mess, but have you ever seen a fly land in a cloud of dust?

If you woke up in the night, what would you do for a light?
Take a feather from the pillow; that's light enough.

On our team, we got very few hits. If anybody reached first base, he had to stop and ask for directions.

A man came home without his key and found all the doors and windows locked. How did he get in?
He raced around the house until he was "all in."

I was on an airline that was so cheap, when they rolled those little steps away, the plane fell over on its side.

Editor to writer: "Your book is a first-grade novel. Unfortunately, most of our readers have gone beyond the first grade."

Crime is really bad in my old neighborhood. On Christmas, Santa Claus comes down the chimney wearing a red suit and a matching ski mask.

My Uncle Newt is as strong as a horse. We just wish he had the IQ of one.

My grandfather always used to ask me, "What's more important, your money or your health?" I'd say, "My health." He'd say, "Great, can you lend me 20 bucks?"

My sister is so skinny, when she wears a fur coat she looks like a pipe cleaner.

My house is such a mess that the neighbors got a petition up against us. Now we all have to wipe our feet before going out.

My barber said, "Why don't you try something different for a change?" I said, "Okay, this time give me a good haircut."

"My teacher sure does like me," a little boy said one day when he came home from school. "I heard her tell another teacher that it was the happiest day of her life when I was promoted to the third grade."

"My father is certainly going to be surprised when I write to him," said the new graduate. "He always said I was so stupid that I couldn't even get a job. And in the last month I've had six."

My neck's as stiff as a pipe, my head's like a lump of lead, and my nose is all stopped up. I don't need a doctor, I need a plumber.

My friend thinks freedom of speech gives her the right to make as many long-distance phone calls as she wants.

My brother went to cooking school and learned how to prepare food in ten greasy lessons.

My uncle died and left me 200 clocks, and I've been busy ever since winding up the estate.

My gym teacher said I could be a real muscle man if I wanted to be. He says I have the head for it.

My doctor told me this operation was absolutely necessary. I said, "For what?" He said, "To send my kids to college."

My mom's cooking is so bad, we have holes in our screen door where the flies go out.

My dad's cooking is so bad, I went into the kitchen once and saw a cockroach eating a Tums.

My doctor is very conservative. If he doesn't need the money, he doesn't operate.

George: Grandma, if I were invited out to dinner, should I eat pie with a fork?
Grandma: Yes, indeed, George.
George: You haven't got a pie in the house that I could practice on, have you, Grandma?

Mother: What are you looking for, Calvin?
Calvin: I'm looking for a dime.
Mother: Where did you lose the dime?
Calvin: I didn't lose it. I just want one.

Bald-headed man: You ought to cut my hair cheaper, there's so little of it.
Barber: Oh, no. In your case we don't charge for cutting the hair, we charge for having to search for it.

Teacher: What would you do if a man-eating tiger were chasing you?
Student: Nothing. I'm a girl.

Mother: How did you come to fall in the lake?
Son: I didn't come to fall in. I came to fish.

Camper: Doctor, that ointment you gave me makes my arm smart.
Camp doctor: In that case, rub some on your head.

Tex: Do fish perspire?
Rex: Of course, what do you think makes the sea so salty?

Christy: Can I have a dollar for a man who's crying outside?
Mom: What's he crying about?
Christy: Ice cream, only a dollar.

Mom: What should I serve with my meat loaf?
Dad: The antidote.

Mother: Dear, go and see how old Mrs. Smith is this morning.
Daughter (after returning): Mrs. Smith says it's none of your business how old she is.

Customer (in department store): Do these stairs take you to the third floor?
Saleslady: No, you have to walk.

Bus driver: What's the matter, sir?
Passenger: I can't stand going up hills. It makes me very nervous.
Bus driver: Then why don't you try what I do?
Passenger: What's that?
Bus driver: Close your eyes.

Orin: There is talk that the next war will be fought with television.
Owen: Well, I'm in training. I've faced some terrible programs.

Rex: When were you born?
Tex: April 2.
Rex: A day too late.

Clem: I have a rare old computer game that once belonged to George Washington.
Slim: But there were no computers back then!
Clem: That's what makes it so rare.

Bill: I dropped a glass on the floor and didn't spill a drop of milk.
Jill: Why is that?
Bill: It was a glass of water.

Farmer: What are you doing in my apple tree, young man?
Boy: Well, sir, the sign says, "Keep Off the Grass."

Dad: Is that young man serious about his intentions?
Daughter: He must be. He asked me how much I make, what kind of meals we have, and how you and mother are to live with.

Larry: Do turkeys have good table manners?
Karry: No. They always gobble at the dinner table.

42

Why was the Swiss yodeler thrown out of the boarding house?
He owed the old lady!

Why is a horse halfway through a gate like a coin?
Because his head's on one side and his tail's on the other.

Why do some monkeys sell potato chips?
Because they're chipmonks.

Why must a doctor keep his temper?
He can't afford to lose his patients.

Why does lightning shock people?
Because it doesn't know how to conduct itself.

Why can't it rain for two days continually?
Because there is always a night in between.

Why do heroes wear big shoes?
Because of their amazing feats.

Why can one never starve in a desert?
Because of the sand which is there.

Why is a crossword puzzle like a quarrel?
Because one word leads to another.

Why did the boy get a dachshund?
Because his favorite song was "Get Along Little Dogie."

Why is an island like the letter T?
Because it is in the middle of water.

Why do Mr. & Mrs. Dumb keep a doormat inside their house?
So when they go outside they don't get the streets dirty.

Why did the robot go mad?
Because he had a screw loose.

Why did Mr. and Mrs. Newbert hire a tutor for their son?
So he could pass recess.

Why did Mr. Dumb tiptoe past the medicine cabinet?
Because he didn't want to wake up the sleeping pills.

Why did the little hummingbird have to stay after school?
He didn't do his humwork.

Why do farmers from Iowa build their pigsties between their houses and their barns?
For their pigs.

Why did the exterminator examine his computer?
He heard there was a bug in the system.

Why do golfers bring an extra pair of pants with them when they play golf?
In case they get a hole in one.

Why would a spider make a good ball player?
Because he is good at catching flies.

Why do you call your dog "Fried Egg"?
Because he rolls over easy.

Why is a river so rich?
It has two banks all its own.

Why did the crow sit on the telephone pole?
He wanted to make a long distance caw.

Why was the little shoe sad?
His father was a sneaker and his mother was a loafer.

Why don't cannibals eat clowns?
Because they taste funny.

What's a good way to keep your house warm?
Put a coat of paint on it.

Why do firemen wear red suspenders?
To hold up their pants.

Why did the farmer put corn in his shoes?
To feed his pigeon toes.

Why does a dog dress warmer in summer than in winter?
Because in the winter he wears a fur coat, while in summer he wears a coat and pants.

Why did the mouse run away from home?
Because he found out his father was a rat.

Why did the man bring a bag of feathers to the store?
He wanted to make a down payment.

Why did the boy keep his bicycle in his bedroom?
He was tired of walking in his sleep.

Why is it hard to remember the last tooth you had pulled?
Because it went right out of your head.

When do chickens have eight feet?
When there are four of them.

When is the toughest time to play horseshoes?
When the shoes are still on the horses.

When is a black dog not a black dog?
When he's a greyhound.

When a car dealer assures you your new car has something that will last a lifetime, what is he referring to?
He is referring to the monthly payments.

When is a cow not a cow?
When she is turned into a pasture.

When is an apple like a book?
When it is red.

When is a clock at the head of the stairs dangerous?
When it runs down and strikes one.

When are you going to open your bakery?
When I can raise the dough!

When is a duck 20 feet tall?
When he's on stilts.

When is a yellow dog most likely to enter a house?
When the door is open.

When a lady faints, what number will restore her?
You must bring her two.

Why should men avoid the letter A?
Because it makes men mean.

Why did the woman spray insect repellent on her computer?
The program had a bug in it.

Why did you put a worm in your sister's bed?
I couldn't find an iguana.

Why was the owl a poor student?
He just didn't give a hoot!

Why does a man permit himself to be henpecked!
Because he's chicken-hearted.

Why does a cow go over a hill?
Because she can't go under it.

Why did the judge sentence the comedian to five years in jail?
He was involved in some funny business.

Why is a horse like a lollipop?
Because the more you lick it the faster it goes.

Why are football players cool?
Because they have a lot of fans.

Why did the robber take a shower before holding up the bank?
He wanted to make sure he'd have a clean getaway.

Why did the worm oversleep?
Because he didn't want to be caught by the early bird.

Why did the dieter bring scissors to the dinner table?
Because he wanted to cut calories.

Why are tomatoes the slowest fruit?
They're always trying to ketchup.

Why did the boy jump in the mud and then cross the street twice?
Because he was a dirty double crosser.

Why are cards like wolves?
Because they belong to a pack.

Why did the football coach send in his second string?
To tie up the game.

Why did the boy hold his report card over his head?
He was trying to raise his grades.

Why is a tent like a baseball?
Because they both have to be pitched.

Where does King Kong plug in his computer?
Anywhere he wants to!

Where did the witch of Endor live?
At Endor.

If you are out of money, where can it always be found?
In the dictionary.

Where is the headquarters of the Umpires' Association?
The Umpire State Building.

Where did the farmer take his pigs on a sunny Sunday afternoon?
On a pignic.

Where was the Declaration of Independence signed?
On the bottom of the page.

Where is paper money mentioned in the Bible?
Where the dove brought the green back to Noah.

Where did Noah keep his bees?
In the ark hives.

Where do salmon go to sleep?
On the riverbed.

Where do fleas go in winter?
Search me.

How many dinosaurs lived on vegetables?
None. They all lived on the earth.

How did the cow feel when she couldn't give any milk?
Like an udder failure!

How can you make 15 bushels of corn from one bushel of corn?
Pop it.

How do we know that a dentist is unhappy at his work?
Because he always looks down in the mouth.

How can you make a pearl out of a pear?
Add L to it.

How did Adam and Eve feel when they left the Garden of Eden?
Put out.

How can a man tell the naked truth?
By giving the bare facts.

A man was locked in a room that had nothing in it except a piano. How did he get out?
He played the piano until he found the right key.

Why did the farmer name his pig Ink?
Because it kept running out of the pen.

Why does an Indian wear feathers in his hair?
To keep his wigwam.

Why should a fisherman always be wealthy?
Because all his business is net profit.

Why did Mickey Mouse take a trip into space?
To find Pluto.

Why does your brother sleep in the chandelier?
Because he's a light sleeper.

Why did the jelly roll?
Because it saw an apple turnover.

Why can't you drive a golf ball?
It doesn't have a steering wheel.

Why is a woman on a deserted island like a woman in a store?
She is always looking for a sail.

Why is your nose not twelve inches long?
Because then it would be a foot.

Why is the letter D like a bad boy?
Because it makes ma mad.

Why is a coward like a leaky faucet?
Because both of them run.

Why does a pig in a parlor resemble a forest fire?
Because the sooner it's put out, the better.

Why is a karate blow like a piece of meat?
Because it is a poke chop.

Why did the boy stand behind the donkey?
He thought he'd get a kick out of it.

Why are false teeth like stars?
Because they come out at night.

Why is a game of baseball like a pancake?
Because they both need batters.

Why should you go to an ironworks to find something you've lost?
Because it's a foundry.

Why didn't the man put an ad in the paper for his lost dog?
Because the dog couldn't read.

Why did the brilliant scientist disconnect his doorbell?
To win the Nobel prize!

What is smaller than an ant's mouth?
His teeth.

How does a crazy person spell farm?
E-I-E-I-O.

How does a musician brush his teeth?
With a tuba toothpaste.

How does a train conductor sneeze?
Ahhhh choo-choo!

How can you recognize crazy rabbit stew?
It has hares in it.

How many actors does it take to change a light bulb?
One hundred. One to change it, and 99 to stand around and say, "I could have done that."

What goes putt-putt-putt-putt?
An over-par golfer.

What do you call someone who steals pigs?
A hamburglar.

What did the sea say to the shore?
Nothing. It just waved.

What two things can you never eat for breakfast?
Lunch and dinner.

How should you greet a German barber?
Herr Dresser.

Why is an ex-boxer like a beehive?
An ex-boxer is an ex-pounder; an expounder is a commentator; a common tater is an Irish tater; an Irish tater is a speck'd tater; a spectator is a beholder; and a bee holder is a beehive.

Which is larger, Mr. Larger or Mr. Larger's baby?
The baby is a little Larger.

What did one elevator say to the other elevator?
I think I'm coming down with something.

Who sings "Love Me Tender" and makes Christmas toys?
Santa's little Elvis.

What is the right kind of timber for building castles in the air?
Sunbeams.

How did the prime minister of Crazyland deal with the problem of Red China?
He bought a pink tablecloth.

Which season do kangaroos like the best?
Springtime!

Where are ankles located?
Overshoes.

Where do fish keep their life savings?
In a riverbank.

What do you call a raccoon that wears bow ties?
Tycoon.

What do you call it when your toes have a good cry?
Football.

Why is E the most unfortunate of all the letters?
Because it is never in cash, always in debt, and never out of danger.

What two numbers multiplied together make 13?
One and 13.

Why shouldn't American girls learn Russian?
Because one tongue is enough for any girl.

What gets lost every time you stand up?
Your lap.

If a soft answer turns away wrath, what does a hard answer do for you?
It turns wrath your way.

How can you tell a Jersey cow from any other cow?
By its license plate.

What is the longest word in the dictionary?
Smiles. There's a mile between the first and last letter.

43

Sign in a power plant
We have the power to make you see the light.

Sign on a vegetable stand
Our corn will tickle your taste buds and make you smile from ear to ear.

Sign on a newly seeded lawn
Your feet are killing me!

Sign in a crazy old-folks home
We're not deaf; we have already heard everything worth hearing.

Sign in a shop window
Wanted: Clerk to work eight hours a day to replace one who didn't.

Sign in a delicatessen window
Come in for a hello and good buys.

Sign in an ice-cream shop
You can't beat our milk shakes, but you can lick our ice cream.

Sign in big store:
Five Santas, No Waiting.

Sign at a reducing salon
Twenty-Four Shaping Days Till Christmas.

Sign on a jewelry shop
Ring Your Christmas Bell.

Sign on an animal shelter
Meowy Christmas and Yappy New Year.

Sign at a community college
If Your Mind Isn't Becoming You, You Should Be Coming Here.

Sign in pet store
Must move—Lost our leash!

Sign in doctor's office
An apple a day is bad for business.

Sign in a garden
Beware of vegetarians!

Sign on cement truck
We dry harder.

Sign on birdhouse
Home Tweet Home.

Sign in loan office window
Come in and borrow enough to get out of debt.

Sign in TV ad in newspaper
Because of the president's speech
"The Invisible Man" will not be seen tonight.

Sign in a service station
We collect taxes—
Federal, State, and Local.
We also sell gasoline as a sideline.

A sign on a garbage truck
Always at Your Disposal.

Sign on board at Al's frankfurter stand
What Foods These Morsels Be.

Elaine: What is it that every child spends much time making, yet no one can ever see it when made?
Elizabeth: I don't know.
Elaine: Noise.

Elaine: What smells most in a perfume shop?
Elizabeth: Beats me.
Elaine: Your nose.

Elaine: What does a stone become when it is in the water?
Elizabeth: I can't guess.
Elaine: A whetstone.

Elaine: What insect runs away?
Elizabeth: I have no idea.
Elaine: A flea.

Elaine: What did the man do when he received a big gas bill?
Elizabeth: You tell me.
Elaine: He exploded.

Elaine: What kind of electricity do they use in Washington?
Elizabeth: I give up.
Elaine: D.C.

Elaine: What turns without moving?
Elizabeth: Who knows?
Elaine: Milk. It can turn sour.

Elaine: What kind of paper makes you itch?
Elizabeth: You've got me.
Elaine: Scratch paper.

Elaine: What is the best way to talk to a skunk?
Elizabeth: My mind's a blank.
Elaine: By long distance.

Elaine: What flower is happy?
Elizabeth: That's a mystery.
Elaine: Gladiola.

Elaine: What did the fish say when he was caught on the hook?
Elizabeth: I'm blank.
Elaine: Gosh! I thought I knew all the angles.

Elaine: What apple has a short temper?
Elizabeth: I don't have the foggiest.
Elaine: A crabapple.

Elaine: What did the fat man say when he sat down to dinner?
Elizabeth: It's unknown to me.
Elaine: I'm afraid this food is going to waist.

Elaine: What gets around people everywhere?
Elizabeth: I'm in the dark.
Elaine: Belts.

Elaine: What are the coldest animals?
Elizabeth: Search me.
Elaine: Mice, because they are three parts ice.

Elaine: What animal disbelieves everything?
Elizabeth: You've got me guessing.
Elaine: Sheep. They always say, "Bah! Bah!"

Elaine: What's the easiest way to get on TV?
Elizabeth: I pass.
Elaine: Sit on your set.

Elaine: What instrument do you use to see monsters?
Elizabeth: How should I know?
Elaine: A horror-scope.

Elaine: What should you do if you wake up in the night and hear a mouse squeaking?
Elizabeth: I don't know.
Elaine: Oil it!

Elaine: What's the difference between the bus and the sidewalk?
Elizabeth: Beats me.
Elaine: The bus fare.

Elaine: What is a country seat?
Elizabeth: I can't guess.
Elaine: A milking stool.

Elaine: What is the best form for a soldier?
Elizabeth: I have no idea.
Elaine: A uniform.

Elaine: What is a parasite?
Elizabeth: You tell me.
Elaine: Something you see in Paris.

Elaine: What drives a baseball batter crazy?
Elizabeth: I give up.
Elaine: A pitcher who throws screwballs.

Elaine: What is a cold war?
Elizabeth: Who knows?
Elaine: A snowball fight.

Elaine: What can a stingy man part with best?
Elizabeth: You've got me.
Elaine: A comb.

Elaine: What would you call a female Indian chief who is always getting into trouble?
Elizabeth: That's a mystery.
Elaine: Mischief.

Elaine: What's the smallest room in the world?
Elizabeth: I'm blank.
Elaine: A mushroom.

Elaine: What branch of the army do babies join?
Elizabeth: I don't have the foggiest.
Elaine: The infantry.

Elaine: What is the best way to drive a baby buggy?
Elizabeth: It's unknown to me.
Elaine: Tickle his feet.

Elaine: What's the happiest day in the life of a young mosquito?
Elizabeth: I'm in the dark.
Elaine: The day it passes its screen test.

Elaine: What headlines do women always notice?
Elizabeth: Search me.
Elaine: Wrinkles.

Elaine: What did the banana do when the monkey chased it?
Elizabeth: You've got me guessing.
Elaine: The banana split.

Elaine: What did the dentist say to the golfer?
Elizabeth: I pass.
Elaine: You have a hole in one.

Elaine: What are fathers from the south called?
Elizabeth: How should I know?
Elaine: Southpaws.

Elaine: What should a fullback do when he gets a handoff?
Elizabeth: I have no clue.
Elaine: Go to a secondhand store.

Elaine: What do you get from a cow with a split personality?
Elizabeth: I don't know.
Elaine: Half and half!

Elaine: What would you get if you mixed a weirdo with a can of beans?
Elizabeth: Beats me.
Elaine: Dork and beans!

Elaine: What was sweet, yellow, and got creamed by Sitting Bull?
Elizabeth: I can't guess.
Elaine: George Armstrong Custard!

Elaine: What do you get if you cross a duck hunter with a parrot?
Elizabeth: I have no idea.
Elaine: A bird that says, "Polly wants a quacker."

Elaine: What do you get if you cross a pig and a cactus?
Elizabeth: You tell me.
Elaine: A porkerpine.

Elaine: What goes around the house peeking through cracks?
Elizabeth: I give up.
Elaine: The sun.

Elaine: What frontier lawman was famous for his indigestion?
Elizabeth: Who knows?
Elaine: Wyatt Burp!

Elaine: What do you call a daredevil flier who makes an emergency landing in the Grand Canyon?
Elizabeth: You've got me.
Elaine: Ace in the hole.

Elaine: What's yellow, fuzzy, and too tired to eat honey?
Elizabeth: My mind is blank.
Elaine: Winnie the Pooped!

Elaine: What did the man say when he drank some poison?
Elizabeth: I don't have the foggiest.
Elaine: This stuff just kills me!

Elaine: What do you call a baseball player who sleeps in the bullpen?
Elizabeth: It's unknown to me.
Elaine: A bulldozer.

Elaine: What do you get if you cross a pony with two dimes and a nickel?
Elizabeth: I'm blank.
Elaine: A quarterhorse.

Elaine: What did one eye say to the other?
Elizabeth: I'm in the dark.
Elaine: There's something between us that smells.

Elaine: What's the best way to get rid of a 100-pound worm?
Elizabeth: Search me.
Elaine: Invite a 1000-pound robin over for breakfast.

Elaine: What do they do if someone eats the stew in the school cafeteria?
Elizabeth: You've got me guessing.
Elaine: Call an ambulance.

Elaine: What do you get if you cross a cat with a cactus?
Elizabeth: I pass.
Elaine: An animal that gives you a pain whenever it rubs against your leg.

Elaine: What do you call a cookbook that gives recipes for using the yellow portion of eggs?
Elizabeth: How should I know?
Elaine: A yolk book.

Elaine: What dog loves to take bubble baths?
Elizabeth: I don't know.
Elaine: A shampoodle!

Elaine: What do you call a deer who's a wimp?
Elizabeth: I have no clue.
Elaine: A namby-pamby Bambi!

Elaine: What did the beaver say to the tree?
Elizabeth: I don't know.
Elaine: It's been nice gnawing you.

Elaine: What would you get if you crossed a fuzzy yellow bear with a virus?
Elizabeth: Beats me.
Elaine: Winnie the Flu!

Elaine: What's a tired tent called?
Elizabeth: I have no idea.
Elaine: A sleepy teepee.

Elaine: What goes "krab, krab"?
Elizabeth: I give up.
Elaine: A dog barking backward.

Elaine: What do you call two bikes that look exactly alike?
Elizabeth: Who knows?
Elaine: Identical Schwinns.

Elaine: What is everyone in the world doing now?
Elizabeth: You've got me.
Elaine: Growing older.

Elaine: What crime did the thief commit in the bakery?
Elizabeth: My mind is blank.
Elaine: A pie-jacking!

Elaine: What do you get if you cross a karate expert with a tree?
Elizabeth: That's a mystery.
Elaine: Spruce Lee.

Elaine: What is the difference between a crazy hare and a counterfeit coin?
Elizabeth: I'm blank.
Elaine: One is a mad bunny, the other is bad money.

Elaine: What kind of snake loves dessert?
Elizabeth: It's unknown to me.
Elaine: A pie-thon, of course.

Elaine: What is a duck's favorite TV program?
Elizabeth: I'm in the dark.
Elaine: The feather forecast.

Elaine: What do you give a seasick elephant?
Elizabeth: You've got me guessing.
Elaine: Plenty of room.

Elaine: What is a frog's favorite drink?
Elizabeth: I pass.
Elaine: Croaka-cola.

Elaine: What's the difference between a gossip and a mirror?
Elizabeth: How should I know?
Elaine: One speaks without reflecting, and one reflects without speaking.

Elaine: What do you call two spiders who just got married?
Elizabeth: I don't know.
Elaine: Newlywebs.

Elaine: What is the difference between a fisherman and a lazy schoolboy?
Elizabeth: I have no idea.
Elaine: One baits his hook, the other hates his book.

45

An editor at a national magazine calls himself "The Fiddler on the Proof."

I have two ducks that I use as an alarm clock. They wake me up at the quack of dawn.

My wife allows no eating in the living room. She's sort of a one-woman food and rug administrator.

Don: Stop acting like a moron.
Dan: I'm not acting.

Customer: Give me two hotdogs—one with ketchup, one without.
Dumb waiter: Which one?

"Oh, no," the waiter exclaimed when he dropped the Thanksgiving dinner. "This means the fall of Turkey, the ruin of Greece, and the breakup of China."

Wife: My husband thinks he's a TV antenna.
Doctor: I think I can cure him.
Wife: I don't want him cured, just adjusted. I can't get channel 47.

Some people call running a 26-mile marathon good exercise. Others call it Christmas shopping.

First it's December with Ho! Ho! Ho!
Then it's January with Owe! Owe! Owe!

Father: Isn't it wonderful how little chicks get out of their shells?
Son: What gets me is how they get in.

She: Where did you get that umbrella?
He: It was a gift from sister.
She: You told me you hadn't any sisters.
He: I know. But that's what's engraved on the handle.

Father: Now I want to put a little scientific question to you, my son. When the kettle boils, what does the steam come out of the spout for?
Son: So that Mother can open your letters before you get them.

Today, car sickness is what you get from looking at the sticker price.

An auction is a place where you can get something for nodding.

My mom's tough. Once when she said "No," I said, "Jimmy's mother always lets him do it." I got sent to my room. Jimmy and his mother got sent to their rooms too.

Who invented the first airplane that didn't fly?
Orville and Wilbur Wrong.

Which is more valuable, a paper dollar or a silver dollar?
The paper dollar because when you put it into your pocket you double it, and when you take it out you find it in-creases.

Who was the first electrician in the Bible?
Noah; he made the ark light on Mount Ararat.

Who's elderly, has many children, and walks around with sticky feet?
The Old Woman Who Lives in the Glue.

Which NFL team would you not entrust with your valuables?
The Pittsburgh Stealers!

Who performs operations at the fish hospital?
The head sturgeon.

Which is heavier, a full moon or a half moon?
A half moon, because a full moon is lighter.

Which has more legs, a cow or no cow?
No cow; a cow has four legs, but no cow has eight legs.

Who writes nursery rhymes and squeezes oranges?
Mother Juice.

Which is correct: The white of the eggs is yellow or the white of the eggs are yellow?
Neither. The whites are white.

Who had big ears, a trunk, and a size 27 glass slipper?
Cinderelephant!

Who killed a fourth of all the people in the world?
Cain, when he killed Abel.

Which is the west side of a little boy's trousers?
The side the son sets on.

Who's gloomy, writes mystery stories, and has a hangnail?
Edgar Allan Toe.

Who earns his living without doing a day's work?
A night watchman.

Which state is round at both ends and high in the middle?
O-hi-o.

Which is better: "The house burned down" or "the house burned up"?
Neither, they are both very bad.

Rustler: You mean you're gonna hang me?
Sheriff: Sure thing. On Monday morning.
Rustler: That's a terrible way to start the week.

Rex: Why did you become a printer?
Tex: I guess I'm just the right type.

Visitor: Do you like reciting, dear?
Child: Oh, no, I hate it, really. But Mummy makes me do it when she wants people to go.

Nathan: Haven't you ever met a girl you cared for?
Noble: Only recently. It was love at first sight.
Nathan: Why don't you marry her?
Noble: I took a second look.

Teacher: If I had two sandwiches and you had two sandwiches, what would we have?
Student: Lunch.

Fox: Say, Beaver, they tell me you can cut down any size tree.
Beaver: Well, I've never been stumped yet.

Did Adam and Eve ever have a date?
No, they had an apple.

It's mostly you I care for. I care for your money only up to a certain point—the decimal point.

Adam: If two wrongs don't make a right, then what do two rights make?
Abner: An airplane.

Dad: If you're good, I'll give you a shiny new penny.
Lad: How about a dirty old nickel?

Customer: Would you mind taking the fly out of my soup?
Waiter: Do it yourself. I'm no lifeguard.

Slim: Say, did you know that most car accidents occur within ten miles of your house?
Clem: In that case, I'm moving to a new neighborhood.

Erika: Your pants look sad today!
Evan: Well, they're depressed!

Bill: What's the difference between a bumblebee and a mattababy?
Jill: What's a mattababy?
Bill: Why, nothing. What's the matter with you?

Dora: In the summer I get up as soon as the first ray of sun comes in my window.
Flora: Isn't that a bit early?
Dora: No, my window faces west.

Animal lover: What do turtles eat?
Animal expert: Bugs.
Animal lover: What kind of bugs?
Animal expert: Slow ones.

She: Tell me the story of the girl who bleached her hair.
He: I never tell girls off-color stories.

Mary: Do you make up these jokes yourself?
Larry: Yes, out of my head.
Mary: You must be.

Daughter: Aw, shucks, Ma. Why do I have to wash my face again before dinner?
Mother: Because you've got a smudge on it, Hon.
Daughter: Why can't I just powder over it like you do?

Bill: I'm not myself today.
Jill: Yeah, I've noticed the improvement.

Waitress: Would you like your coffee black?
Customer: What other colors do you have?

Big sister: What did you learn in school today?
Little brother: Algebra.
Big sister: Say something in algebra.
Little brother: Pi r squared.
Big sister: No, no! Pie are round, cornbread are square!

Husband: Where is yesterday's newspaper?
Wife: I wrapped the garbage in it.
Husband: Darn it! I wanted to see it.
Wife: There wasn't much to see—just some orange peels and coffee grounds.

Bert: Do you think anyone can predict the future with cards?
Curt: My mother can. She takes one look at my report card and tells me what will happen when my father comes home.

Justin: Did you know that Daniel Boone's brothers were all famous doctors?
Julius: No.
Justin: Don't tell me you've never heard of the Boone Docs?

Edgar: A snake bit me.
Eldon: Put something on it.
Edgar: I can't—it slithered away.

Juliet: Romeo, Romeo, where art thou?
Romeo: Down here in the bushes—the trellis broke!

Have you ever heard of a baby raised on elephant's milk?
Yes, a baby elephant.

Clint: Have you been to Cape Kennedy?
Flint: Yes, it's a blast!

Norris: If you had a choice, would you rather be in a collision or an explosion?
Boris: A collision.
Norris: Why?
Boris: Because in a collision, there you are. But in an explosion, where are you?

First sheep: Baa-a-a
Second sheep: Moo-o-o
First sheep: Moo-o-o? Why do you say Moo-o-o?
Second sheep: I'm learning a foreign language.

Overheard: Jerry and I are going to have a secret marriage. Jerry doesn't even know about it yet.

Arnold: Did you know that bowling is the quietest sport?
Burt: No—how can that be?
Arnold: You can hear a pin drop!

Orin: Know what I'm going to be when I graduate?
Owen: A senior citizen?

Edna: Don't you think they make a perfect couple?
Elsie: Yes, I do. He's a pill, and she's a headache.

Randy: I'm nobody's fool.
Florence: Well, maybe someone will adopt you.

First explorer: Look! Here's a lion's track!
Second explorer: Great! You find out where he went, and I'll find out where he came from.

First actress (behind the scenes): Did you hear the way the public wept during my death scene?
Second actress: Yes, it must have been because they realized it was only acting!

46

Knott and Shott fought a duel. The result was that they changed conditions: Knott was shot, and Shott was not. It was better to be Shott than Knott.

Jimmy Jack Hackett jilted Jill Brackett.

Rotten Roscoe rescued Rosie from the roaring rapids.

Rub rugs roughly.

Landlubbers love blubber.

Shameful sheep-sellers sell cheap sheep.

A swim well swum is a well-swum swim.

Three free-thinking frogs think friendly thoughts.

Trim these three fine free trees.

The sixth sick sheik's sixth sheep's sick.

47

He was so dumb—when he earned his varsity letter, someone had to read it to him.

Boss: Why are you so late?
Worker: I overslept.
Boss: You mean you sleep at home too?

I don't know why it's so important to finish your homework. As soon as you get it done, they just give you more.

Bob: I'll have you know, I have royal blood in my veins.
Jim: Whose? King Kong's?

The other night a Chicken Delight truck came to the door. I went to answer it, but a mouse pushed me aside and said, "That's for me."

The only reason some people are lost in thought is that they're total strangers there.

Boss: Did you put those circulars in the mail?
Secretary: No, sir. I couldn't find any round envelopes for them.

Singer: Did you notice how my voice filled the whole room tonight?
Friend: Yes, a lot of people had to leave to make room for it.

Albert: I hear your brother fell into an upholstery machine.
Amanda: Yes, but he's fully recovered now.

Voice on the phone: Is this the game warden?
Game warden: Yes, it is.
Voice: Thank goodness, I have the right person at last. Would you please give me some suggestions for a child's birthday party?

Archibald: Waiter, there's a fly in my pea soup.
Waiter: There's nothing to worry about, sir. I'll take it back and exchange it for a pea.

Husband: I gave you a mink coat for Christmas, and you still weren't satisfied.
Wife: You know I'd rather have a Cadillac than a mink.
Husband: Sure, but where can I get an imitation Cadillac?

When do you know you're getting old?
When by the time you've lit the last candle on your cake, the first one has burned out.

Math teacher: Roderick, if I had ten quarters in my left pocket, ten dimes in my right, and ten nickels in both of my back pockets, what would I have?
Roderick: Heavy pants.

Sister: Willie broke the front window, Mommy.
Mother: How did he do that?
Sister: I threw a baseball at him, and he ducked.

Wealthy man: I'll have to fire my chauffeur. He's nearly killed me twice.
Friend: Don't be too hard on him. Give him one more chance.

Every night the dog brings my dad his pipe, his slippers, and the newspaper. For the next half-hour we all sit around and try to figure out which is which.

Our family dog is a good judge of people too. My sister came home with one date, and the dog took the family car and drove to Pittsburgh.

Will February March?
No, but April May.

A man walks into a restaurant and orders a cup of coffee. When it arrives, he pours the coffee into an ashtray and eats the cup and saucer, leaving only the handle on the table. He then calls the waiter over and orders more coffee. As each cup arrives, he pours out the coffee and eats the cup and saucer. Pretty soon, there's nothing but a pile of cup handles in front of him. He turns to the waiter and says, "You think I'm crazy, don't you?"
The waiter replies, "Yes, sir. The handle's the best part!"

Mrs. Lilley: Noel, go outside and water the garden.
Noel: But Mom, it's raining.
Mrs. Lilley: So put your raincoat on.

Don: This coffee is terrible.
Waitress: Young man, I've been making coffee since before you were born.
Don: Well, I sure wish you hadn't saved it for me.

Eskimo Bill: Where does your mom come from?
Eskimo Bob: Alaska.
Eskimo Bill: Don't bother. I'll ask her myself.

Customer: This shop is a disgrace. I can write my name in the dust on this furniture.
Assistant: It must be wonderful to have an education.

What did Grandma do when she received a letter from her grandson saying he had grown another foot since she had last seen him?
She knitted another sock.

The problem with most parents today is that they give their kids a free hand...but not in the right place.

Boss: Did your supervisor tell you what to do?
New employee: Yes, sir. He told me to wake him up if I saw you coming.

Convict: Writing your memoirs?
Cell mate: No, just a letter to myself so I'll get some mail.
Convict: What are you saying?
Cell mate: Don't know. Mail call isn't until 3:30.

Nicky: Look at that couple over there arguing. Boy, he sure is henpecked.
Vicky: How can you tell? They're not speaking. They're using sign language.
Nicky: Yes, but just look. He can't get a finger in edgewise!

First jail-breaker: How did you get rid of the bloodhounds that were trailing us?
Second jail-breaker: I just threw a penny in the stream, and they followed the cent.

Biff (twice nicked by the barber's razor): Hey barber, gimme a glass of water.
Barber: What's wrong, sir? Hair in your mouth?
Biff: Naw, I wanna see if my neck leaks.

What letter is a drink?
T.

Customer: Do you have bacon and eggs on your menu?
Waiter: No, sir, we clean our menus every day.

I show a different face to everyone, but I have no face of my own. Who am I?
A mirror.

Billy: How many sides does a circle have?
Willie: Two—the inside and the outside.

Friend: Was your uncle's mind vigorous and sane up to the very last?
Heir: I don't know. The will won't be read until tomorrow.

Stern parent: Willie, I'd like to go through one whole day without once scolding or punishing you.
Willie: Well, Mother, you have my consent.

Molly: What nationality are you?
Polly: Well, my father was born in Iceland and my mother was born in Cuba.
Molly: Oh, so you're an Ice Cube?

Car dealer: This car has had just one careful owner.
Buyer: But look at it—it's a wreck.
Car dealer: The other five owners weren't so careful, I have to admit.

My mom doesn't push me to clean my room too much. Straightening my room is such a gigantic project, I would probably have to drop out of school to do it.

At a convention of egotistical chess players in Fresno, the air conditioning failed, and they were told to sit in the hall where more air was circulating.
The manager of the hotel was heard to complain to an employee, "I'm so tired of listening to a bunch of chess nuts boasting in an open foyer!"

McCalley, the star fullback of a Mississippi college football team, got a job in the post office during the Christmas holidays. He was assigned to sorting letters, and he got quite good at it. In just one day, the fullback had become the fastest letter sorter in post office history.

The local postmaster was quite pleased and said to McCalley, "Son, you are the fastest letter sorter I ever did see. You could have a great future with the post office, if you are interested."

"Thank yew," said the fullback. "Tomorrow, ah'll try tew do even betta. Ah'll try tew read the addresses."

What this country needs...

...a safety net for people who jump to conclusions.

...a transmission that will shift the blame.

...a good no-scent cigar.

...a song for unsung heroes.

Husband (shakily as he brings home flowers for his wife): The florist was held up by an armed robber. You might describe the man as a petrified florist.

Before the plane took off, the flight attendant handed out gum. "This will prevent your ears from popping as we climb."

After the flight, everyone left the plane but one little old man.

"Why are you still here?" the attendant asked.

"You'll have to speak up!" the old man yelled back. "I can't hear very well with this gum in my ears!"

Three-year-old Paul came home from Sunday school and asked his mother and father to sing "Silent Night" over and over again.

His parents were puzzled by his fascination with the song, until they listened carefully as the boy sang, "Silent night, holy night. Paul is calm, Paul is bright."

Husband: My wife served a beautiful meal last night. Meat loaf in one corner of the plate, mashed potatoes in another corner of the plate, and brussel sprouts in another corner. She has to put them all in separate corners so we can tell them apart.

A Special Christmas Carol

Jingle bells,
Spending swells,
Charge cards all the way.
Oh, what fun it is to shop,
Until you have to pay!

Jeff: Go wash your face, Susie. I can see what you had for breakfast this morning.

Susie: I bet you can't.

Jeff: Sure I can. You had eggs.

Susie: Ha, ha. No, I didn't. That was yesterday!

Husband: Something just has to be done about the cost of this year's Christmas trees. My neighbor bought one for 15 dollars and his wife is wearing it as a corsage.

Ed: I hear the men are striking.
Jeff: What for?
Ed: Shorter hours.
Jeff: Good for them. I always did think 60 minutes was too long for an hour.

Nick: Have you heard what they call the new employee?
Rick: No, what do they call him?
Nick: Chocolate bar. He's half nuts.

Arty: The tornado that blew my father's car away left another in its place.
Smarty: Must have been a trade wind.

Professor: I say there, you in the automobile. Your tubular air container has lost its rotundity.
Driver: Huh?
Professor: I said the cylindrical apparatus which supports your vehicle is no longer symmetrical.
Driver: What?
Professor: The elastic fabric surrounding the circular frame whose successive revolutions bear you onward in space has not retained its pristine rotundity.
Driver: Eh?
Passing boy: Hey, mister, he says you got a flat tire!

Proud mother: Baby Ben is a year old now, and he's been walking since he was eight months old.
Bored listener: Really? He must be awfully tired.

Annie: One time my father shot an elephant in his pajamas.
Frannie: How did the elephant ever get into your father's pajamas?

Friend: So your daughter now drives a car? How long did it take her to learn?
Broke father: About two-and-a-half cars!

Phil: Do you know what happened to the plant in the math class?
Bill: No, what?
Phil: It grew square roots.

Len: Gee, I'm depressed.
Glen: But why should you be if your girl said she'd be faithful to the end?
Len: Because I'm the halfback!

Simon: Why did the joker take his bread and butter out in the street?
Frank: I don't know.
Simon: He wanted to find a traffic jam.
Frank: Did he find it?
Simon: Yes, a truck came along and gave him a big jar.

Two turtles stopped to get a drink in a drugstore. When they ordered their sodas it started to rain. The big turtle said, "Go home and get an umbrella." The little turtle said, "Don't drink my soda while I'm gone."

Two years later the big turtle said, "I guess he isn't going to come back. I might as well drink it." A voice from outside said, "If you drink the soda, I won't go home."

48

What's in a Name?

What do you call a guy who likes to change oil in cars?
Derek.

What do you call a guy who repairs wheels?
Axel.

What do you call a guy who likes all kinds of cars?
Otto.

What do you call a guy who is accident prone?
Rex.

What do you call a guy who sleeps on the leaf pile?
Russell.

What do you call a guy who can't light firecrackers?
Dudley.

What do you call a guy who fell ten floors from a building and landed on his head?
Spike.

What do you call a guy who loads trucks?
Van.

What do you call a guy who's been attacked by a lion?
Claude.

What do you call a guy who likes to read road maps?
Miles.

What do you call a guy who plants rice?
Paddy.

What do you call a girl who is very sickly and pale?
Ashley.

What do you call a guy who likes to wear all types of hats?
Cap.

What do you call a guy who ties ribbons for a living?
Beau.

What do you call a girl who is happy all the time?
Cher.

What do you call a girl who likes to work in the garden?
Fern.

What do you call a girl who is very interested in Gypsies?
Crystal.

What do you call a girl who likes to eat sweets?
Candy.

What do you call a girl who has very attractive eyes?
Iris.

What do you call a guy who's been dropped into the middle of the ocean?
Bob.

What do you call a guy who's been thrown across the surface of a pond?
Skip.

What do you call a guy who's been hung up on the wall by his belt?
Art.

What do you call a guy who changes tires?
Jack.

What do you call a guy who uses a shovel all the time?
Doug.

What do you call a guy who everyone hangs pictures on?
Wally.

What do you call a guy who delivers the mail?
Bill.

What do you call a guy who smells like a cow?
Barney.

What do you call a guy who likes meat, potatoes, and vegetables?
Stu.

What do you call a guy who falls asleep on your front porch?
Matt.

What do you call a guy who is a lookout for the Coast Guard?
Seymour.

What do you call a guy who hits a baseball over the fence?
Homer.

What do you call a guy who eats mustard all the time?
Frank.

What do you call a girl who stands next to walls?
Lena.

What do you call a girl who gets caught in a fence?
Barb.

What do you call a girl who stands on one foot?
Eileen.

What do you call a girl who makes hamburgers?
Patti.

What do you call a girl who is in charge of the woman's movement?
Libby.

What do you call a girl who likes fine furniture and jewels?
Tiffany.

What do you call a girl whom you can't seem to get rid of and keeps coming back?
Penny.

She was born on her parents' wooden anniversary so they called her "Peg."

49

"If you refuse to go out with me," said the boy with intensity, "I shall die."

She refused.

Eighty-five years later he died.

I was going to straighten my room yesterday, but I couldn't find the rake and shovel.

I really like New Year's Day. It's the only day of the year that I'm not behind in my homework.

Bruce: Have you any meat for my dog?

Butcher: Only a lamb's foot.

Bruce: He'll like that—he's a sheepdog.

Exercise and diet are the best ways to fight hazardous waists.

Old judge: It would appear that the defendant is not telling the truth.
Defendant: Why's that, sir?
Old judge: Well, you told the court that you have only one brother, but your sister says that she has two brothers.

A lady visiting an orchard was amazed at the amount of fruit. "What do you do with all this fruit?" she asked the farmer.
"We eat what we can, and can what we can't," he replied.

There is a secret Christmas message in the following letters. Can you find it? A, b, c, d, e, f, g, h, i, j, k, m, n, o, p, q, r, s, t, u, v, w, x, y, z.
No L (Noel).

Do big ships like the Titanic sink very often?
No, only once.

In a young boy, what is cleanliness next to?
Impossible.

On which side does a fish have the most scales?
On the outside.

In a beauty contest, what do you look for?
Because I like to.

No matter how smart you are, there is one thing you will always overlook. What is it?
Your nose.

From what dairy do people in the Sahara Desert get their milk?
Dromedary.

Which bird is the lowest-spirited?
Bluebird.

Which Indian was in charge of facial tissues?
The hankie-chief.

Alfred: Grandpa, what do I have to know to teach my sister Clara tricks?
Grandpa: More than Clara.

Husband (looking up from his newspaper): There's a story here that says there's a man run over on New York City streets every eight minutes.
Wife: That's awful. Someone should tell him to stay on the sidewalk.

While taking a cruise in the Arctic, Mrs. Cross suddenly pointed across the ocean and said, "Look! An iceberg!"
Mr. Cross looked and looked where she was pointing, but he didn't see a thing.
"Obviously, darling, you have a problem," said Mrs. Cross.
"What problem is that?" he asked.
"Poor ice sight," she replied.

Retirement is when you finally have the time to sink your teeth into something fun...but you don't have the teeth.

Father: At a family picnic when I was 12, I ran off with the circus.
Son: Gee, was it fun?
Father: I don't know. The police made me bring it back.

I'm really unlucky. My parents bought me a wristwatch that's waterproof, shock-proof, and rust-proof. I had it three days and it caught fire.

Well, I wouldn't say that Mrs. Jones has a big mouth, but every time she smiles she gets lipstick on her ears.

Boss: An hour late again! What's your excuse this time?
Barney: I was sideswiped by a cross-town bus!
Boss: And I suppose you're going to tell me that took an hour?

What do you do if your elephant squeaks?
Give it some peanut oil.

Smith: I hate paying my tax bill.
Brown: You should pay up with a smile.
Smith: I've offered them a smile, but they insist on money.

One kid in our class was always in trouble. I won't say his parents were called into school often, but his mom and dad had the lead in the school play.

There was an apple, a potato, and a banana on the Empire State Building. The apple and the potato jumped off. Why didn't the banana jump?

Because the banana was yellow.

Joe: There's one name on the committee whom I've never heard of.

Moe: Oh, that's probably the person who actually does the work.

Willie was invited to a party, where refreshments were bountifully served.

"Won't you have something more, Willie?" the hostess asked.

"No, thank you," replied Willie, with an expression of great satisfaction. "I'm full."

"Well, then," smiled the hostess, "put some fruit and cakes in your pockets to eat on the way home."

"No, thank you," came Willie's rather startled response. "They're full too."

An old gentleman clad in a somewhat youthful suit of light gray flannel sat on a bench in the park enjoying the spring day.

"What's the matter, Sonny?" he asked a small urchin who lay on the grass and stared at him intently. "Why don't you go and play?"

"Don't want to," the boy replied.

"But it is not natural," the old gentleman insisted, "for a boy to be so quiet. Why don't you want to?"

"Oh, I'm just waitin'," the little fellow answered. "I'm just waitin' till you get up. A man painted that bench about 15 minutes ago."

A little girl sitting in church watching a wedding, suddenly exclaimed: "Mummy, has the lady changed her mind?"

"What do you mean?" the mother asked.

"Why," replied the child, "she went up the aisle with one man and came back with another."

A man threw a nickel toward the blind man's cup. The coin missed and rolled along the pavement, but the man with the dark glasses quickly recovered it.

"But I thought you were blind!"

"I am not the regular blind man, sir," he said. "I'm just taking his place while he's at the movies."

Psychologist: How many ears does a cat have?

Patient: Two.

Psychologist: And how many eyes does a cat have?

Patient: Two.

Psychologist: And how many legs does a cat have?

Patient: Say, Doc, haven't you ever seen a cat?

Stan: I have a baseball dog.

Duncan: Why do you call him a baseball dog?

Stan: Well, he catches flies, chases fowls, and runs for home when he sees the catcher coming.

Bill: Is a chicken big enough to eat when it's two weeks old?

Granny: Of course not.

Bill: Well, then how does it manage to live?

Customer: Those apples you sold me yesterday were awful. They tasted of fish.

Grocer: That's not surprising. They were crabapples.

They advertise a soup that will put color back in your cheeks. They don't tell you that the color is green.

Girl: I wouldn't marry you if you were the last person on earth.
Boy: If I were, you wouldn't be here!

He generally has more food running down his chin than most other people have on their plate.

His favorite pastime is sitting on the sidewalk and watching cement harden.

Why did Mr. Dumb move out of his house?
Because he heard most accidents happen at home.

What is sunbathing?
A fry in the ointment.

Maybe the grass looks greener on the other side of the fence because they take care of it over there.

When is a girl like a mirror?
When she is a good-looking lass.

Lady visitor: What a beautiful mountain! There must be many romantic stories connected with it.
Mountaineer: Yep, two lovers went up that mountain and never came back here.
Lady visitor: My, my, what ever became of them?
Mountaineer: Went down the other side.

Once upon a time there were three men on their way home from work. The first man, passing a deserted shack, saw a ten-dollar bill on the ground. He was about to pick it up when he heard a voice say, "This is the voice of Daniel Boone. Touch that money, and it'll be your doom."

The man left the money and ran away.

The second man came by, heard the voice, and he, too, ran away.

Then the third man walked past. He picked up the money, and the voice said, "This is the voice of Daniel Boone. Touch that money, and it'll be your doom."

The third man said, "This is the voice of Davy Crockett. This ten-dollar bill goes in my pocket!"

Farmer: I'd like some 4 by 2's.

Clerk: We only have 2 by 4's.

Farmer: That's okay. We can turn them around.

Clerk: How long do you want them?

Farmer: Oh, we want them for a long time. We're going to build a house.

Tom: Your overalls are all wet.

Pete: I know, I just washed them.

Tom: Then why are you wearing them?

Pete: Because the label says: Wash and wear.

Fred: My uncle has the laziest rooster in the world on his farm.

Bill: How can you tell?

Fred: Well, he never crows at sunrise. He just waits until some other rooster does, and then nods his head.

Voice on the phone: Is this Joe?
Joe: Sure, this is Joe.
Caller: Doesn't sound like Joe.
Joe: It's Joe, all right.
Caller: Can you loan me $10, Joe?
Joe: I'll ask him as soon as he comes in.

A business executive decided to ask a few friends the question, "How's business?" Their answers:
Astronomer: Looking up.
Author: Mine seems to be all write.
Butcher: We're making ends meat.
Tobacconist: Going up in smoke.
Exterminator: We're gradually getting the bugs out.

Nick: First I got tonsillitis, followed by appendicitis and pneumonia, ending up with neuritis. Then they gave me hypodermics and inoculations.
Rick: Boy, did you have a hard time!
Nick: I'll say. I thought I'd never pull through that spelling test!

Ann: Why did Linda take a hammer to bed with her?
Diane: I don't know. Why?
Ann: So she could hit the hay.

Two boys were arguing about what their fathers were able to do.
Said Billy, "You know the Atlantic Ocean? Well, my dad dug the hole for it."
"That's nothing," replied Gary. "You know the Dead Sea? Well, my dad is the one who killed it."

Three men in a smoking compartment of a train were discussing the vagaries of men. One said, "I know a man who writes very small to save ink."

Another said, "A friend of my father always stops the clock at night to save wear and tear on it."

"Your men are spendthrifts," said the third. "I know an old man who won't read the paper because it wears out his glasses."

Modern Mary

Mary had a little lamb
Given her to keep.
It followed her around until
It died from lack of sleep.

In what month do girls talk the least?
February.

Snob: My ancestors came over on the Mayflower.
Slob: That was lucky for them. Immigration laws are stricter now.

Cindy: Do you see that boy over there annoying Sue?
Frank: Sure, but he isn't even talking to her.
Cindy: That's what's annoying her.

In marble walls as white as milk,
Lined with a skin as soft as silk,
Within a fountain crystal clear,
A golden apple doth appear;
No doors there are to this stronghold,
Yet thieves break in and steal the gold.
What am I?
An egg.

50

What do liars do after they die?
They lie still.

Boy: I have an idea.
Girl: Beginner's luck!

Caller: Hello, operator, I would like to speak to the king of the jungle.
Operator: I'm very sorry. The lion is busy.

Dick: Every morning I take my dog for a tramp in the fields.
Mick: Does the dog enjoy it?
Dick: Yes, but the tramp's getting rather fed up.

With stars in her eyes she asked, "Is this a real diamond ring?"
He: It better be or I've been cheated out of 29 cents.

The kids were playing cowboys. The front porch became the "Last Chance Saloon." The first boy strolled up to the first step. "I'll have a rye," he said. Second boy followed him, "I'll have a whole wheat."

Have you heard about the new doctor doll? You just wind it up and it operates on batteries.

Can you think of anything worse than a hippopotamus with bad breath?

Can you name a carpenter's tool you can spell forward and backward the same way?
Level.

Can you spell "blind pig" with two letters?
Pg (pig without an eye).

I am something that every living person has seen, but no one will ever see again. What am I?
Yesterday.

I am something that always weighs the same, whether I am larger or smaller. What am I?
A hole.

There were three dry-cleaning stores on one block in a big city, and the competition for business was quite fierce. At last, one of the stores put up a big sign in the window: "Best Dry-Cleaners in the City."

About a week later, the second store blossomed forth with a bigger sign: "Best Dry-Cleaners in the World."

And a week after that, the third store put up a modest little sign: "Best Dry-Cleaners on the Block."

Boss: The first thing you should know about the job is it pays $50 a week.

Applicant: Why, that's an insult!

Boss: But we only pay every two weeks, so you're not insulted as often.

There are seven maple trees and on the seven maple trees are seven branches and on the seven branches are seven acorns. How many acorns are there?

None. Acorns don't grow on maple trees.

Baby corn: Mommy, who brought me?

Mother corn: The stalk brought you!

Lady in a pet shop: How much is that canary?

Clerk: Five dollars.

Lady: Good. Send me the bill.

Clerk: Can't do that, lady. You have to take the whole bird!

Mother: Who gave you that black eye?

Johnny: Nobody gave it to me. I had to fight for it.

Allan: Tom was arrested for stealing a pig.
Dick: How did they prove it?
Allan: The pig squealed.

Ron: Hi, Mom, I'm home.
Mother: Where have you been?
Ron: I had to stay after school again.
Mother: For crying out loud!
Ron: No, for laughing out loud.

Have you heard about the man with five legs?
His trousers fit him like a glove.

A farmer couldn't tell his two horses apart, so he tried cutting the tail off one horse. This was no good because the tail grew right back. Then he cut the mane off the other horse. This didn't work either, because the mane grew back. Finally he measured them and found that the white horse was two inches taller than the black horse.

Did you hear about the two cement mixers that got married? Now they have a little sidewalk running around their house.

Mack: What did the Pilgrims come over on?
Jack: The Mayflower.
Mack: What did the midgets come on?
Jack: Shrimp boats.
Mack: And what did the doctors come on?
Jack: Blood vessels.

Little Evie: Don't you like to play with paper dolls anymore?
Little Ernie: No. I cut them out long ago.

Have you heard of the new pet shop in Greenwich Village?
Yes, it's called, "Fish and Cheeps."

Jack: My roommate makes life unbearable. He keeps six sheep and five goats in the bedroom and it smells terrible.
Mack: Why don't you open the window?
Jack: And let all my pigeons escape?

"Isn't it disgusting the way some people drive? Just look how close that lunatic ahead of us is driving."

Jack: I haven't had any sleep for nine days.
Mack: That's terrible!
Jack: Fortunately, I don't have any trouble sleeping nights.

Visitor: You used to have two windmills here. Now, I see you only have one.
Farmer: There was only wind enough for one so we took the other one down.

Two detectives were standing over a dead man named Juan.
First detective: He was killed with a golf gun.
Second detective: What's a golf gun?
First detective: I don't know, but it sure made a hole in Juan.

Rick: Why'd you stop going steady with Lisa?

Nick: She's got her heart set on being a schoolteacher, you know, and when I didn't show up the other night she asked me to bring a written excuse signed by my mother.

Joe: Is your dog trained?

Moe: Well, when I tell him not to sit up—he doesn't sit up.

A young lady stalled her car at a traffic light one winter day. She cranked the starter, tried again, and choked her engine. All the while, an impatient citizen behind her honked his horn steadily. Finally she got out and walked back.

"I'm sorry, but I don't seem to be able to start my car," she told the driver of the other car pleasantly. "If you'll get up there and start it for me, I'll stay here and lean on your horn."

Sign over umbrella stand: "This umbrella belongs to the champion heavyweight fighter of the world. He is coming right back."

Five minutes later there was a new sign: "Umbrella is now in possession of the champion marathon runner of the world. He is not coming back!"

Jones: Do you believe in free speech?

Smith: Certainly!

Jones: Splendid! May I use your telephone?

Joe: Did you know that Kendall gave his wife a 300-piece set of dishes for Christmas?

Moe: That was very nice of him.

Joe: Well, it was only supposed to be 24 pieces, but he tripped coming home from the store.

Everybody in the neighborhood hates this one grouchy neighbor. They say she has the only house on the block with a two-broom garage.

Not-very-smart Elliot walked into a pet shop.
Elliot: How much are those kittens in the window?
Clerk: Thirty dollars apiece.
Elliot: How much for a whole one?

We had a kid in our class who spent so much time in the principal's office, they gave him his own key.

Mom says my room looks like a cyclone hit it, but that's not true. If a cyclone hit it, it would be neater.

Sunday school teacher: Class, what do you know about Adam's wife, Eve?
Bartholemew: They named Christmas Eve for her.

Gerald: I just love the holiday season!
Jack: Yeah, I always get a little sentimental about Christmas. In fact, every Christmas Eve I take off my socks and stand them in front of the fireplace.

What do you get when you cross a dog and a hen?
You get a pooched egg.

One year I received 286 Valentine's cards. I would have gotten more, but my hand got tired writing out my address.

A good pickpocket can remove your wallet with the skill of a surgeon… though he won't make as much money.

This one restaurant we went to used to make soup that was so greasy, if you sprinkled salt and pepper on it, they slid right off.

Jeff: What kind of toothpaste do you use?
Larry: I don't use any.
Jeff: How come?
Larry: My teeth aren't loose.

Roy: There are at least 25 girls at my school who don't want to go out on a date.
Troy: How do you know?
Roy: I asked them.

Marsha: There's no need for me to change the way I look. All the boys like me just the way I am.
Horace: Right—single.

Man: I saved my wife a lot of standing in line this Christmas. I didn't give her a present.
Friend: How's that?
Man: I gave her an exchange certificate. Who needs a middleman?

It is better to give than to receive a Christmas gift because you don't have the bother of exchanging it.

"Your church certainly has an innovative pastor, Miss Prudence."

"Yes, we certainly do! Last Christmas Eve he decorated the front doors of our church to resemble a wrapped holiday gift. His sign read: Please Open Before Christmas."

Dan: Why'd you tell everyone I'm stupid?

Don: I didn't know it was a secret.

Ever notice that the people who say "That's the way the ball bounces" are usually the ones who dropped it?

One girl in our class is so neat she always parts her hair perfectly straight. That's fine, but in her eyebrows?

Blessed are those who hunger and thirst, for they are sticking to their diets.

Melba: I knew a hen who laid a two-pound egg. Can you beat that?

Pam: Yes, with an egg beater.

One year I got a strange Valentine. It said: "I've always admired you from afar. Stay there."

I straightened up my room once and found a younger brother I never knew I had.

I once bought a rabbit's foot for good luck. It kicked me.

Diner: Every time I have a cup of tea, I get a stabbing pain in my right eye. What shall I do?
Waiter: Take the spoon out of your cup.

Diner: What's your soup like today?
Waiter: Just like it was yesterday—only a day older.

Diner: Waiter! This London broil tastes like an asphalt shingle!
Waiter: Sorry, sir, meat prices have simply gone through the roof.

Diner: Waiter, where should we sit to be served quickly?
Waiter: How about at the restaurant next door?

Diner: Waiter, why have you got your thumb on my steak?
Waiter: I don't want it to fall on the floor again, sir.

Lady: How much is a cup of coffee?
Waitress: Fifty cents.
Lady: How much is a refill?
Waitress: Free.
Lady: I'll take a refill.

Diner: Waiter, I'm still waiting for the turtle soup I ordered.
Waiter: Well, sir, you know how slow turtles are.

Diner: Waiter, I've reserved a table. I'm giving dinner for all my friends tonight.
Waiter: Oh, you must be the table for two, sir.
Diner: I didn't come here to be insulted.
Waiter: Why, where do you normally go?

Diner: Waiter, this fish is bad.
Waiter: You naughty fish, you!

Diner: Waiter, this food gives me heartburn.
Waiter: Well, what did you expect—sunburn?

Diner: I don't like this piece of cod. It's not half as good as the one I ate here two weeks ago.
Waiter: Well it should be—it's from the same fish.

Diner: Waiter, these eggs are awful.
Waiter: Don't blame me. I only laid the table.

Why don't they let crazy people operate elevators?
They forget the route.

How do amoebas break up with their girlfriends?
They split.

Name two people who were never wrong.
Wilbur and Orville Wright.

What colors would you paint the sun and the wind?
The sun rose and the wind blue.

When a librarian goes fishing, what does she use for bait?
Bookworms.

What did one horse say to the other?
I can't remember your mane, but your pace is familiar.

Why should a man never tell his secrets in a cornfield?
Because there are too many ears there, and they might be shocked.

Which is the best side of the bed to sleep on?
The top side.

How can you be sure the engine in your car isn't missing?
Lift the hood and look.

Where does a crazy Ken doll grill his hamburgers?
On a Barbie-cue.

How can you tell if your lawn is sick?
When you hear the grass mown.

When the baby cries at night, who gets up?
The whole neighborhood.

Why are oysters lazy?
Because they are always found in beds.

What is a stupid ruler called?
A ding-a-ling king.

What two letters got kicked out of the alphabet for being rotten?
D-K.

Why do hummingbirds hum?
Because they can't remember the words.

How many people does it require to take a picture off a wall?
Ten. One to hold the picture and nine to knock down the wall.

Who changed King Tut's diapers?
His mummy.

I have ears, but I can't hear. What am I?
A cornstalk.

What do most people give and few people take?
Advice.

Where do king crabs live?
In sand castles.

What is the difference between an elephant and a flea?
An elephant can have fleas, but a flea can't have elephants.

How do you remove varnish?
Take out the letter R and make it vanish.

What is the value of the moon?
Four quarters.

What is the difference between a mouse and a young lady?
One harms the cheese, and the other charms the he's.

How does a crazy person fan himself?
He holds his hand still and waves his face in front of it.

What kind of sentence would you get if you broke the law of gravity?
A suspended one.

What has never killed anyone, but seems to scare some people half to death?
Work.

What did the mother ghost say to the baby ghost when they got in the car?
Fasten your sheet belt.

Who is the oldest whistler in the world?
The wind.

Do chickens jog?
No, but turkeys trot.

Why didn't the baby get hurt when he fell down?
Because he was wearing safety pins.

Which shoes are made for lazy people?
Loafers.

Was Ben Franklin surprised when he discovered electricity?
Oh yes, he was shocked.

When shad swim in schools, who helps out the teacher?
The herring aide.

What happens when the bridge of your nose collapses?
Nose drops.

Do shad sing?
Only when they have musical scales.

Why did the shrimp blush?
Because someone saw it in the salad dressing.

Why is an empty purse always the same?
Because there is never any change in it.

If one horse is shut up in a stable and another one is running loose down the road, which horse is singing "Don't Fence Me In"?
Neither! Horses can't sing.

What do you call a veterinarian with laryngitis?
A hoarse doctor.

If a cannibal ate his mother's sister, what would he be?
An aunt eater.

How do you cheer a basketball player?
Hoop, hoop, hooray!

What day of the year is a command to go forward?
March fourth.

Who invented the telephone and carries your luggage?
Alexander Graham Bellhop.

What is the best way to keep a skunk from smelling?
Hold his nose.

What kind of jokes does a scholar make?
Wisecracks.

What is the best day to fry food?
Friday.

What two opposites mean the same thing?
Half-full and half-empty.

What makes more noise than a pig in a sty?
Two pigs.

Which fruit is always sad?
Blueberries.

I have leaves, but I'm not a plant. What am I?
A table.

What's hard-boiled and can bench press 600 pounds?
Arnold Schwarzenegg.

What is the difference between an engineer and a teacher?
One minds the train, while the other trains the mind.

What do you do with a blue monster?
Cheer him up.

What country makes you shiver?
Chile.

What do you call the secret instructions for opening a zipper?
A zip code.

Why was Cleopatra so hard to get along with?
She was the queen of denial.

Other Books by Bob Phillips

The All-New Clean Joke Book

The Awesome Book of Bible Trivia

The Awesome Book of Heavenly Humor

Awesome Good Clean Jokes for Kids

The Best of the Good Clean Jokes

Dude, Got Another Joke?

Extremely Good Clean Jokes for Kids

Fabulous & Funny Clean Jokes for Kids

Good Clean Jokes to Drive Your Parents Crazy

How Can I Be Sure?

How to Deal with Annoying People

Jammin' Jokes for Kids

Laughter from the Pearly Gates

Over the Hill & On a Roll

Over the Next Hill & Still Rolling

Over the Top Clean Jokes for Kids

Slam Dunk Jokes for Kids

Squeaky Clean Jokes for Kids

Super Cool Jokes and Games for Kids

Super-Duper Good Clean Jokes for Kids

A Tackle Box of Fishing Funnies

The World's Greatest Collection of Clean Jokes

The World's Greatest Knock-Knock Jokes for Kids

The World's Greatest Wacky One-Line Jokes

For more information, send a self-addressed stamped envelope to:

Family Services
P.O. Box 9363
Fresno, California 93702